WEALTH BUILT

# WEALTH BUILDING WITH
# *Franchising*

*Creating generational wealth by
following a proven system*

COMPILED BY
# LINDA BALLESTEROS

Copyright © 2023 by Linda Ballesteros

All rights reserved. No part of this publication may be reproduced, distributed, or transmitted in any form or by any means, including photocopying, recording, or other electronic or mechanical methods, without the prior written permission of the publisher, except in the case of brief quotations embodied in critical reviews and certain other noncommercial uses permitted by copyright law. For permission requests, write to the publisher, addressed "Attention: Permissions Coordinator," at the address below.

www.mpowerfranchiseconsulting.com
Linda@MpowerFranchiseConsulting.com

Ordering Information:
Quantity sales. Special discounts are available on quantity purchases by corporations, associations, and others. For details, contact the publisher at the address above.

Printed in the United States of America

Book Production
Marvin D. Cloud, mybestsellerPublishing.com

First Edition

To all the dreamers, hustlers, and visionaries who are not afraid to pursue their goals and create their own success stories. This book is for you. You have the power to transform your life and achieve wealth beyond your wildest imagination. I hope this book inspires you, motivates you, and guides you on your journey to financial freedom. Remember, the only limit is your own mind.

You can do it!

# CONTENTS

**FOREWORD By Red Boswell**.................................................................ix

**Chris Severs** ........................................................................................ 1
A Wealth Abundance Mindset:
Releasing fear and claiming success

**Heath Falzarano** ............................................................................... 17
Baseball, Rollercoasters and Then There is Wealth

**Dr. Tom DuFore**................................................................................ 27
Building Wealth by Franchising Your Business

**Schuyler "Rocky" Reidel** ................................................................ 37
Multi-Unit Franchise Ownership
The key to unlocking generational wealth

**Greg Aguirre** ..................................................................................... 53
Maximizing Wealth
The synergy of franchise ownership and commercial real estate investment

**Toni Harris Taylor** ........................................................................... 69
From Quitting to Legacy

**David & Laura Greenwood** ........................................................... 83
Make a great living while making a difference

**Linda Ballesteros** ............................................................................. 99
Seeking Full Spectrum Wealth

# FOREWORD

By Red Boswell
*President of International Franchise Professional Group*

Hey there, fellow Freedom-Seeker!

Are you tired of the mundane nine-to-five grind? Do you dream of financial freedom and the ability to live life on your own terms? If so, then you're in for a treat! *Welcome to Wealth Building With Franchising,* a book that will open your eyes to the incredible opportunities that await you in the world of franchising.

If you're holding this book in your hands, chances are you're looking to build wealth and create a better future for yourself and your loved ones. And guess what? You're in the right place! Linda Ballesteros has put together an incredible resource that will show you how to achieve your financial goals through the power of franchising.

Franchising has become a proven path to wealth creation for many individuals. It offers a unique business model that allows aspiring entrepreneurs like you to leverage the success and systems of an established brand, while still maintaining the independence and flexibility of owning your own business. It's like having the best of both worlds! But why should you consider purchasing a franchise? Well, let me tell you, there are plenty of compelling reasons. First and foremost, when you invest in a franchise, you're buying into a proven business model with a track record of success. Unlike starting a business from scratch, where you have to figure out everything on your own, a franchise provides you with a roadmap to follow, reducing the risks and uncertainties that come with entrepreneurship.

Another significant advantage of franchising is the support and resources that come with it. Franchise companies often provide comprehensive training, ongoing support, and access to a network of fellow franchisees who can offer guidance and advice. You're never alone in your business journey when you're part of a franchise system. Plus, many franchises have established marketing and advertising programs that can help you attract customers and grow your business faster than you could on your own.

But wealth building with franchising is not just about financial success; it's also about creating a fulfilling and meaningful life.

As a student and leader in franchising for over two decades, I value unwavering integrity above all else —and you should too. It's obvious throughout *Wealth Building With Franchising* that Linda and her contributors believe, as I do, that integrity is at the core of a successful and fulfilling life. Customers expect consistency and quality from a franchise, and upholding those standards is essential to building a successful and reputable business. This book highlights how integrity should be at the heart of every decision you make as a franchisee, from choosing the right franchise to operating your business with honesty and transparency. As you read, you'll learn how operating a franchise with integrity, by adhering to the values and principles of the brand, can contribute to your long-term success, happiness *and* finances.

Now, you might be wondering how to find the perfect franchise opportunity that aligns with your financial and lifestyle goals. That's where franchise consultants, or as Linda calls them, "matchmakers," come into play. These experts are like your personal advisors, helping you navigate the complex world of franchising and identifying the best opportunities that match your skills, interests, and investment level. They can save you time, effort, and money by guiding you through the franchise selection process, conducting due diligence, and negotiating the best terms for your franchise agreement. Linda highlights the benefits of working with franchise consultants and how they can be a valuable resource in your journey towards financial freedom through franchising.

*Wealth Building With Franchising* covers a wide range of topics that will empower you to make informed decisions and take strategic steps towards financial success. The chapters are filled with practical advice, real-life examples, and insights from industry experts, including Tom DeFore, Founder of Big Sky Franchising, Schuyler "Rocky" Reidel, renowned Franchise Attorney, and Greg Aguirre, CEO of Capital Rivers Commercial (franchise partner and investor). The experience and contributions shared by these franchising veterans make this book a trusted source of invaluable wisdom. From learning how to franchise your own business and unlock generational wealth through multi-unit ownership, to maximizing your wealth through synergies between franchise ownership and commercial real estate investment, this book covers it all. But it's not just about the money. You'll see that franchising can also be a way to make a difference in your community and have a positive impact on society. Franchise ownership can provide opportunities for job creation, community involvement, and philanthropic efforts.

Finally, *Wealth Building With Franchising* encourages you to seek full-spectrum wealth. Wealth is not just about financial success, but also about achieving work-life harmony and ultimately, the life of your dreams!

membership@ifpg.org
https://www.linkedin.com/in/redboswell/

**Franchise Wire**

> Incredible change happens in your life when you decide to take control of what you have power over instead of craving control over what you don't.

—**Steve Maraboli**

# CHRIS SEVERS

LifeMastery Consultant
https://dreamsinbloomllc.com/
dreamsinbloomllc@gmail.com
Chris.Severs@DreamsInBloomLLC.com

832-377-7092

Book an appointment now
https://dreamsinbloomllc.com/book/

Chris Severs is the owner of Dreams In Bloom LLC. As a certified LifeMastery Consultant with the Brave Thinking Institute: The Premiere Training Center for Transformational Coaching, Chris can help you create a life that you love living. Chris specializes in helping Entrepreneurs and Business owners build their dreams, accelerate their results and create richer, more fulfilling lives.

For over six years, Chris has studied and implemented transformational success principles, and as a sought-after speaker, trainer, and certified coach, Chris' workshops and coaching programs help people break through limitations and achieve greater results than they've known before. If you're looking to gain clarity, confidence, and achieve your next level of success, while enjoying the highest levels of fulfillment in life, Chris's coaching programs can help you get there.

Email Chris at Chris.Severs@DreamsInBloomLLC.com to learn more about how you can achieve your dreams and create a life you truly love living.

# A Wealth Abundance Mindset: Releasing Fear and Claiming Success

Working in corporate America can be hard and exhausting. Especially when working long hours and usually shifts that do not allow for a work life balance. I understand this all too well during my experience in corporate America.

After attending Hospitality and Travel School, I quickly started my corporate career in 1988 working for Braniff Airlines. I was young and naïve, but I jumped in and began to fall in love with the fast and exciting pace of the travel industry. Getting to travel the country, meeting people and experiencing a variety of cultures was so exciting. I spent the next 30 years working in the travel industry and worked in several capacities, trying to get ahead and move up.

After a few management roles, I decided that I didn't want a management position because I found I was working longer and harder than the frontline employees I managed. The more I advanced, the more I became disappointed. Still not finding the happiness I was looking for, I finally decided to accept a frontline position and be happy because I didn't see any other way to get out.

I did this kind of work for many years. I would keep telling myself that the job was making me sick and very unhappy and realized I would die a quick death if I didn't make a change. How many times have you said the same thing to yourself about your job? How many times, have you again and again, made excuses for yourself and kept on going with the same job?

The excuse I used was "this is all that I know," or "I don't have the training to get out and do anything else." Sure, I could go back to school, but I didn't have the time to invest in myself. Does this sound familiar?

While I was chatting with a friend the other day, they told me about how they had to rush one child to school and the other to the doctor and then hurry back to work so the boss wouldn't yell at them for missing work again. This kind of stress can be enough to drive anyone crazy.

Another issue is if you have a family to feed and keep a roof over their heads, you definitely don't have the time to spend taking more classes because you can barely spend any time with family as it is.

How many times have you missed a child's ball game, piano recital, or a holiday with the family? How many times have you arrived home so late that you were not able to eat dinner, or maybe you just threw a frozen dinner in the microwave because you were just too tired to cook?

You always seem to be in a hurry to take the kids to school, get to work, and get back home. By the time you get home you are so exhausted you fall in bed and collapse and have no family time.

Where is the work-life balance with this kind of schedule? Are you one who sits at your desk every day asking yourself *why am I doing this? What is this job giving me? I keep coming to work, day in and day out, but get nowhere. I seem to be on a merry-go-round.*

Or maybe you are someone who must work two or maybe even three jobs and are still not able to make ends meet. Maybe you juggle your finances to pay for a child's medicine this month and then pay a past due electric bill from last month. The cycle seems to never end, and you keep thinking, *how do I get out of this rat race? Or will I just sit here and die while working at this desk?*

Your health will be affected by these work forces, with the stress on the body, and stress on the brain. The stress will cause your muscles to tighten which can lead to back, neck, and shoulder pain. The stomach becomes so upset and tight that it can develop ulcers because of this ongoing lifestyle. If you continue without a change, it will for sure lead to more serious and deadly health issues.

Considering all of this, you may feel like you have gotten stuck in the riptide of corporate America and that you are not able to see any other choice. If you have had any of these thoughts, you are not alone. These situations sound depressing, and they are. I was right there, just like you, having those same kinds of thoughts. I felt the same way asking the same questions.

As I talk to people, I keep hearing these scenarios over and over from individuals who are at their wits end and feel there is no way out. The good news is there is hope, because life is full of choices. You must first decide enough is enough. Then think about what you would love. This is your first step to creating the dream life.

As a Life Mastery Consultant, I empower people to make these kinds of changes in their lives, by supporting them in deciding to take a stand against what has become familiar. This familiar place has lulled them into believing that this is all there is, but I help them create a dream for something they would love.

It may be a new dream job or maybe starting their own business. Whatever their dream, they can definitely make a change to get something more out of life than what they have been settling for.

Life is not meant to be lived by just settling for something others tell you is possible. You make a change by changing your thinking. I invite people to start making a change by adopting a thinking pattern of gratitude. Be grateful for what you currently have. You may not like everything that you have, but you must be grateful for what it is teaching you. You will start by just noticing what you are thinking. You know that thoughts cause feelings, because if you think scary thoughts your heart will beat faster. And when you think negative thoughts, you will feel down and depressed.

Now if you find yourself thinking negative or angry thoughts, just stop take a breath and change your thoughts to something you would love or something you are grateful for. When you decide to make a change, it doesn't have to be a big change, because a small change for the positive can have long lasting positive results and lead to even greater results. I say, "Start from where you are, with what you have."

Start by looking at the dream job you have always thought about doing or start researching that business you have wanted to start. Just take one step that you know could lead you in the direction of getting what you want in life and out of that stuck pattern that you have been accepting. You must go out and create what you would love.

So why not design a dream life? Most of us have often been told if we want something we must work harder to get it and to stop daydreaming. Well, I am here to tell you, "Dream Big!" Dream as big as you can possibly think. Do not think of what others will say or what society might say is possible, dream full out for something that you would love. Pick something that makes you come alive when you think of it and start writing it down.

I love the following quote:

"Don't ask yourself what the world needs. Ask yourself what makes you come alive, and go do that, because what the world needs is people who have come alive."
—**Howard Thurman**

## The first principle in the Dream Builder program is Designing your Dream

Just like you would do if you were building a house, you sit down with the builder and give specifics of what it is you want in this house. And just like building a house, you want to be as clear as possible and with as much specificity as possible for your dream. You will write this dream as though it is happening now. Start writing your dream by saying "I'm so happy and grateful now that..." and continue writing your dream. I invite people when they are writing their dream to focus on four areas of life.

These are Health and Well-being, Love and Relationships, Vocation, and Time and Money Freedom.

You will want to have a dream in all four of these areas of life. Then once you have written your dream, you'll write "this or something better still." This will signal to life that you are open to something greater than what you can think of right now. Now once you have written this dream, you'll look at it and say, yeah that is a life that I would love. You'll have a feeling of "I can do this." And you can.

## The second principle in the Dream Builder program is Deciding for Your Dream

Of course, if you are going to decide for something that you would love, you want to make sure you are in love with this dream. This dream will make you come alive when you think about it. When you are building your dream, you will start to evoke a feeling of, "Oh yeah, I can live this life." Without making a firm decision for what you would love, you will have hesitancy and confusion.

This kind of thinking will slow you down and can even push your dream away. You will not be able to stay focused and clear on the dream. When you make a firm decision for your dream, you are signaling to life that you are ready to step into something new that you have dreamed up. You will make this decision without knowing the "HOW."

The "HOW" is not important at this stage; that will be revealed when you are ready. With this dream you have just dreamed up, you are not going to know everything that you need to know in order to bring this dream about. If you did know how to bring this dream about, you would have already done so. You'll need to dream bigger. It is our human nature wanting to know the "HOW," when we start something.

Some of us want to know every step in the process, before we decide. Now this doesn't mean you have to jump headfirst into this new endeavor, however, some people do make that leap of faith all at once. You are the one who gets to make this decision, so do what feels right to you.

Some people feel they must sever all ties of the old in order start something new. But others can work with the current situation and start to work on a transition to the new dream. Just don't create more stress for yourself. Now starting something new will naturally cause some fear. Whatever way works best for you is what I invite you to do.

Fear of the unknown can be stressful, and it will talk to you by saying things like "what are you thinking," "who do you think you are," "you've never done anything like this before." This is okay, but don't let it stop you from deciding for your dream. This fear is just a limiting belief or paradigm of your current reality. You are dreaming bigger than what you have lived before. So yes, there is going to be some fear.

"F.E.A.R. is False Evidence Appearing Real."
**– Oprah**

## The third principle in the Dream Builder program is Befriending Your Fear

Yes, that is correct. You will befriend your fear by using this fear as fuel to help propel you towards your dream. If you don't have some fear of the new endeavor and have the discontent of your current circumstances, you will not be able to pull yourself away from the current life of familiarity. There is always a magnetic pull to the familiar.

Therefore, some people stay stuck in the same patterns year after year, because they get comfortable with the familiar and are too afraid to make any changes. You can call this being more in love with your drama, than in love with your dream. You can start by changing how you think of fear. Just tell yourself, this fear is my jet fuel that is propelling me towards my dream. If you are thinking about starting your own business, do *not* do it alone. Get support like a mentor or coach to help guide you.

Most all professional athletes have a mentor and coach to help them see where they need improvement, and you'll need to do the same to be successful. A mentor can help by giving you encouragement and inspiration that you might be missing. A coach can help you see beyond your current circumstances and situation and guide you into a more positive way of thinking.

Some people get caught up in current circumstances where they get stuck and start to lose steam. A coach can see this and help you navigate through the thought process. In a franchise business, you can get a mentor who has already been down this road and will help you avoid pitfalls and stumbling blocks. If you are starting something from scratch, in today's world there is most usually a group of people with similar experiences that can help and encourage you through the process. You can think of these mentors and coaches like training wheels on a bike. When you first started to ride a bike, you most likely started with training wheels. They helped you gain the balance you need to have a stable ride. A mentor and coach can do the same thing for you in business.

If you should stumble when you are beginning your business, do not give up. Just use this experience as a learning tool, then pivot and try something new so that you can keep going. Never stop or give up. You are more powerful than you realize, and you have the knowledge and power to create anything you can dream up. You may not know exactly every step, but if you can dream it up, you can certainly make it come about.

I have been studying these principles since 2016. But experience using these principles came in a big way in 2019 when the company that I worked for at the time had just been bought by a much larger company and was changing processes. I was told that all front-line employees were going to have to work different shifts, for example, nights, weekends and split shifts. I had not worked this type of shift work in about fifteen years, and it was not going to fit my lifestyle now. I had just gotten engaged, and this kind of schedule was out of the question. I just couldn't believe this was happening to me and I kept asking "Why, why, why?"

After being miserable and experiencing lots of frustration for a few weeks, I decided to leave the company. I was afraid and apprehensive as I made this decision because I had never left a job without having something to go to. However, I made a firm decision and put in my two weeks' notice and left on that Friday having a feeling that I would be okay.

By the next Tuesday, I had another job offer. This new job was in a totally different industry than I had ever worked before, and it had much better hours and more flexibility. I was shocked at how quickly this happened, but I knew I was on the right track.

Then the pandemic hit, the company started laying off workers, but I was one of the few who was spared and kept right on working throughout the pandemic. I was very grateful for my job and that I was still working, however, during this time, I found myself searching and longing for more fulfillment. I found that I was not feeling fulfilled in what I was doing, and I needed more.

So, I kept asking myself what I would love, and then one day, seemingly out of the blue I received a call about a program that I was taking, and they asked me if I had ever thought of being a life coach. I had not thought of this, but I have always wanted to help others, and most of my career was in service to others. So, after hearing about being a life coach, I really resonated with this process and how it helps others, and quickly joined the program.

I eventually became a Certified Life Mastery Consultant with the Brave Thinking Institute, which is the Premier Life Coach training company in the world. Once I was certified, I quickly started my business Dreams In Bloom LLC, then I began attracting clients where I witnessed their transformation and successes. This expanded my passion for helping others, and I knew that I had stepped into my soul's purpose. I had found my calling in life. When you step into your soul's purpose, you will know this is where you are supposed to be. I was so excited seeing my clients' transformation using these principles.

One of these clients was Theresa, who was retired and on a fixed income. When Theresa came to me, she was skeptical of the program. She had tried other programs and self-help books, however nothing she did got her the results that she was looking for. I got very clear with her on our initial strategy session, where we found out what she wanted out of life, what her dream life would look like, and what her hobbies were. We found that her hobbies were painting and making jewelry.

I instinctively asked her, "Have you ever thought of selling your jewelry or paintings?"

"Oh, my goodness no," she said. "I could never do that. I'm not good enough. I just make it for myself and for family. It's just soothing for me."

This was my clue that Theresa had some limiting beliefs about herself. One area that I focus on with everyone that I work, is the ability to see themselves as way more powerful than they realize.

We all have within us the power to create anything we desire. We must believe in ourselves. We most usually will doubt our abilities because we falsely believe we are not good enough, not good looking enough, don't have the education or experience, and so on. These are all limiting beliefs that have been instilled in us by society, family, and culture. These limiting beliefs must be addressed so that we can start installing a new positive thought pattern about ourselves.

Once we start installing new thought patterns, we find that our whole perception about life changes. What seemed to be important is no longer important and we need to release what no longer serves us.

With Theresa, we went to work on different areas of her life. About six weeks into the program, I asked her how her painting was going.

She said, "You're never going to believe this."

I asked, "What?"

She said, "A friend of mine came to my house and saw a painting that I had finished, and said they would love to have this painting."

I said, "If you want it, here it is."

The very next week she received a call from a person her friend had spoken to about the painting. This person was a real estate broker and had called Theresa to invite her to be a part of an art show, where she along with 29 other artists would be showing their art. Having the limiting belief that she wasn't good enough, Theresa was afraid and nervous about the process.

She said, "Oh my god, I can't do this."

I said, "Why not?"

She said, "I'm not good enough, what if they don't like my painting?"

I asked, "Why aren't you good enough? Someone liked your painting, and I am very sure there are others that will like your paintings as well."

So, with that fear she made a bold decision to step into the opportunity and participate in the art show. By making this bold decision she went and had an amazingly fun time meeting and talking to the attendees and other artists, and she sold over $700 of her art that day. After that show Theresa was asked to do a commissioned painting that would double her first art show amount. She could not believe how amazing this process can be. This was confirmation for her that when you change your thinking and you decide for your dream, you step into the opportunities that are presented. Doing it afraid. About four weeks later I was speaking with Theresa, and she told me that she had been asked to be a part of another art show. Do not underestimate the power of your thinking. Our thinking can either be our best friend if we train ourselves to think correctly, or it can be our worst enemy if we just go along with normal everyday thinking.

This is one story of many I could share. I can briefly tell you my own story where I am living a life that I love in business, in love and relationships, in health, and time and money freedom. This is so much better than my life prior to 2016, where I was lying in bed, depressed and hating life. These principles are designed to help anyone achieve a positive result through a positive thought process.

They are based on the idea that our thoughts create our reality, and that by changing our thoughts we can change our lives. Through these principles, you will learn how to recognize and reframe negative thoughts, how to create positive affirmations, and how to use visualization to manifest your goals. You will also gain the skills to help you stay positive, even in difficult times. These principles work, when you apply them to your life.

I love my life and you can love your life, too.

It starts by deciding for what you would love.

# HEATH FALZARANO

https://www.naturals2go.com
https://www.linkedin.com/in/heath-falzarano-5110431b5/

Heath Falzarano is the president, majority shareholder, and owner of Naturals2Go, the flagship Healthy Vending business opportunity brand of Vendtech International, Inc. Heath graduated from the State University of New York at Cortland with a Bachelor of Arts in Physical Education. From 1993-1997, he was a four-year starter and captain of the baseball team. He also earned 30 postgraduate credits toward a Master of Education in Special Education from Mansfield University in Pennsylvania in 1998–1999. From 2000–2006, Heath worked as a special education teacher in upstate New York. He modified the curriculum in grades pre-k through 12 to accommodate students with disabilities. Heath moved to Buffalo in 2006 and met his wife there. In addition to his current position as president of Vend Tech International, Inc., which he has held since 2018, Heath has owned and operated a vending business through Naturals2go from 2016 to the present, as well as a Lead Generation call center from 2012 to the present.

## Baseball, Rollercoasters, and Then There is Wealth

These three things may appear unrelated to some, but for me there is an extremely strong link between them. Some may find it difficult to see any connection between seemingly unrelated topics, however, for me they are specifically all intertwined.

At the dinner table as a child growing up, topics of money, wealth or possessions were not areas of discussion. We simply didn't talk about it. My family and I had spent most of my formative years discussing topics such as sports, family, and other activities. I was born in a very small rural community. I did not come from money, but I always felt "rich" in my surroundings and with people that cared about people.

I use the word rich in quotes, as the term rich or wealth for me is not about money and possessions, but more about the joy in your life based on the person you are, who you surround yourself with, and the experiences you encounter along the way. Nonetheless, over the course of my life, I have made some good and bad moves, met some amazing and some not so amazing people, all of which were utterly essential to this story and my journey.

My name is Heath, I am a former teacher and coach, I am a husband, and proud father of two, and the president and owner of Naturals2go Healthy Vending business opportunity. Most people consider our company a franchise, we are very similar less certain fees and royalties. I have been asked to share my thoughts on wealth and will do that in the next 1500 words or so. I do not consider myself a writer and was extremely flattered to be asked to be a part of this book. I will share a few concepts, tell a few stories, in that maybe you can share or relate to some of what I have experienced.

The concept of wealth, which many people can describe in their own unique ways, has recently piqued my interest. Mostly, on how people choose to define it. People from various backgrounds have different ideas about what constitutes wealth or prosperity. Different people use a multitude of terminology when referring to the concept of wealth, and it always makes me curious, right, or wrong in my definition, but to hear others' ideas around wealth and what it means in their world.

In my mind, the term "wealth" does not refer to financial well-being, possessions, or accomplishments. Instead, "wealth" denotes an abundance of something else, it has multiple meanings at once. I have chosen to define wealth, in my world, as the concept of learning and choosing joy through experiences. Essentially, I feel in my terms, that wealth is synonymous with the ability to be happy and joyful, even when you may not be experiencing those feelings in that moment.

The opportunity to have experiences is what most will fail to venture into. I often refer to this as "mental wealth." Another way to think about mental wealth is as having a large mental toolkit, based on your surroundings, your experiences, and surrendering to the fact that you get to choose, define, and respond to any circumstance you are presented with. I believe what I've learned from my surroundings, as well as the new information I seek out on a regular basis, has provided me with invaluable insights. These insights centers around the creation of freedom of choice, being present in the moment, having joyful experiences, being a part of a positive team, and surrounding yourself and your family with good people that have amazing spirits. I have been lucky to be given these insights, and I make it a point to keep myself in the present on a regular basis, and to take advantage of every moment. Because of my consistent efforts to learn new things and broaden my curiosity, I believe that these opportunities have been provided to me. I am convinced that curiosity and experiences have been directly proportional to the amount of effort I've put in.

Lessons learned from my experience with baseball have helped me define and understand wealth. I've discovered that playing baseball as a young boy and through college, and running a successful business have many parallels. Both require a great deal of effort, preparation, and dedication. This is true not only on the playing field, but also in everyday life. Baseball has taught me a plethora of valuable life lessons that have helped shape my character. I will frequently lean back to my definition of wealth and share that it has been drastically molded through my baseball experiences. Hitting in baseball is one of the most difficult skills any sport. As a matter of fact, if you are a lifetime 300 hitting in the big leagues you're a likely to be in the hall of fame. To note, a 300 hitter is only successful thirty percent of the time, and that should tell you something about the difficulty of hitting a baseball. There is a moment in baseball, specifically from a hitter's standpoint that is strongly connected to wealth and learning.

You may have heard the saying, "live life like a 3-1 count." A 3-1 count is a fantastic pitch count to get to if you are a hitter. Essentially, it's that moment when you are prepared and reach that count, it's your opportunity to smash the next pitch. The pitcher is at a slight disadvantage because he doesn't want to walk you and he is forced to throw a strike. If you are prepared in that moment to take full advantage of the opportunity and not let the ball go by, you could get a nice fastball right over the plate. Frankly it's the best time to swing for the fences. The batter must choose whether or not to swing at the next pitch. Being able to "swing for the fences" and seize opportunities as they arise in business necessitates confidence and boldness. To be fearless and confident enough in business is to "swing for the fences."

When you are playing baseball, and chasing your dreams in business ownership, you must be ready to take a swing at any time. It's critical to be prepared mentally to take that swing whenever the situation arises it. The first step toward achieving this goal is to develop the proper mindset, which is then followed by consistent preparation. Mindset and consistent preparation, I believe these are great tools that have helped me build "wealth."

Every pitch is a strike, until it isn't. This is another experience I learned from my time playing baseball that has resonated me the most since I stopped playing. This is just one of the many valuable lessons I've gained from playing baseball, which has taught me so much about life in general. In other words, you should always enter any at-bat believing you can hit the ball, even if you later discover that you cannot. Even if the ball turns out to be too high for you to hit, this concept remains true. I was lucky enough to have some amazing college coaches, and one concept that was shared in the mindset and preparation of hitting, is that "every pitch is a strike, until it's not."

This mindset is just as important in business as it is in sports, the arts, or any other field. Its significance is the same in each of these universes. I believe this positive preparation in sports has carried over into my business, and my term for wealth building. The opposite of course, is to not be prepared and potentially miss all opportunities. My father would call it being more on the offensive side of the game.

In business we call it, preparation, and seizing the moment for opportunities because we believe in so many. Achieving your objectives is far more likely if you approach each new opportunity with the confidence that you can capitalize on it. As a result, your chances of reaching your objectives will improve. This confidence will greatly increase your chances of success in a shorter period. You will fall short at times, but that doesn't mean you shouldn't keep trying and believing in yourself. It is critical that you stay the course. Even though you will undoubtedly fail at times, your long-term success is dependent on your focus and readiness to swing for the fences and seize the moment.

Acquiring wealth can be a physically demanding endeavor that requires the same tenacity and determination as a sport like baseball. The two tasks are equally difficult, however the effort required to complete each of these tasks is roughly comparable. A batter who has been in a hitting slump is always one pitch away from getting out of that slump. This is because the more times a batter is up, and with the proper mindset, and of course skill, the more likely the batter will break the slump. A business owner must be mentally prepared for both good and bad times in their company's history. Nonetheless, it's critical to keep your mind clear and to stay on track throughout the process, learn as much as possible from your mistakes and to continue living your life despite a setback. It's also critical to take away as many valuable lessons as possible, I would call this the cement of building wealth.

Now let's talk about rollercoasters. The thrill of a roller coaster ride comes from the anticipation of terrifying moments such as steep drops and corkscrews. I remember as a kid the first time I had an opportunity to ride a legit rollercoaster. The knots in my stomach making the long journey to get on the 60 second ride was probably worse than the ride. I remember getting locked in the roller coaster and as it made its slow clicking sound to the top before its straight drop down, I could feel my heart beating through my chest. Well, the ride turned out amazing; it was over before I knew it. My fear turned to excitement, as I rushed to get back in line and do it again. Taking calculated business risks can be as terrifying as riding a rollercoaster. If you let it get to you, well the fear of it, will cause you to miss the opportunity. One of my parents said to me before I went on, "Just keep the bar down, and it will all be fine." That stuck with me for some time, especially in building business, and wealth. It can get scary, and doubtful at times, but embarking on these journeys, just like riding that roller coaster for the first time, is so worth it, and I frequently hear that whisper to "keep the bar down and it will all be good." Remember that if it were simple and beneficial, everyone would do it.

Everything that builds who you are, never comes at the right time, nor does it even care how you feel about it. Going on journeys to better yourself and others, you must confront and overcome irrational fears while also pushing yourself outside of your comfort zone. Only in this manner does one stand a chance of ever becoming and gaining some "mental wealth." You must be prepared for the inevitable ups and downs of business, which are akin to riding a rollercoaster. It's easy to become distracted by the view from the rollercoaster's peak and forget that the ride is about to descend sharply. When you've reached the apex of the ride, it is important to keep your accomplishments in check and remain focused.

To make this work, you must also ignore distractions and keep your mind focused on the underlying goals of your actions. Concentrate on the causes of your decisions rather than the consequences. Consider what inspired you to take the steps you're taking right now. Concentrate on the reasons that drove you to take the actions you're taking right now. In business, it's critical to remain steadfastly committed to your ultimate goals despite the inevitable setbacks. In this sense, you must be unwaveringly committed to your own vision and refuse to allow yourself to be sidetracked by obstacles that lie in your path. If you want to be a professional, you must keep moving forward and not let anything stop you. The ability to maintain perspective is proportional to your ability to weather the inevitable ups and downs of running your own business. If you can accomplish this, you will be more resilient in the face of adversity. If you can accomplish this, you will be in a better position to face the challenges that lie ahead in your journey towards wealth.

    I have enjoyed every experience that life through baseball and rollercoasters have offered to me. When you seek to create wealth, look back to your past and discover what life has already given you. Really define what the meaning of "wealth" is within your world. Having the opportunity to live, and journey every day, as well as choosing your own definitions for any circumstances, is what really should excite people. Most will make excuses or wait to feel a certain way before they decide to act in the moment or take the leap. It's never going to feel right, and it will be nerve racking at times. If you're not prepared to swing for the fences, it will simply pass you by. Be present and in the moment. I am here to tell you, it can be a ton of fun, full of experiences that you will keep forever. Go for it, be something special to others, dare to step into what you want, and remember, "Just keep the bar down, and it will all be fine."

# DR. TOM DUFORE

Big Sky Franchise Team
www.BigSkyFranchiseTeam.com
tom@bigskyfranchise.com

855-8-BIG-SKY(855-824-4759)

Dr. Tom DuFore is the founder and CEO of Big Sky Franchise Team. He is an author, entrepreneur, franchise expert, and host of the "Multiply Your Success" podcast. Big Sky Franchise Team is an award-winning consulting firm specializing in helping growth-minded entrepreneurs franchise their businesses. Tom and Big Sky have advised more than 600 companies, including Jamba Juice, Two Men and A Truck, Matco Tools, and many others.

Tom values building up owners looking to franchise their business as well as members of his team. His leadership focuses on treating people with respect, encouraging them to be their best, and always learning. He seeks to live out his company's purpose to "Inspire and Foster Greatness" through three core values: Win-Win Relationships, Professional Excellence, and Continuous Improvement.

He earned his Doctor of Business Administration (DBA) degree and he is a Certified Franchise Executive. Tom is happily married with three children.

# Building Wealth by Franchising Your Business

If you could exit out of the day-to-day operations of your business *and* retain all of your intellectual property and income, would you?

For many people, the answer is "yes." The reality of making such a scenario a reality is much closer than you think and can be done through the implementation of franchising. Franchising your business provides a multiplying effect for increasing wealth and impact and allows you to create an exit strategy. The following gives an overview of franchising, how you make money as a franchisor, why franchising your business makes sense, the Triple Win Formula, and how you can create an exit strategy through franchising your business.

**The Basics: What is Franchising?**

Think of franchising as being kind of like a car lease. When you lease a car, there is an explicit agreement stating that you are allowed to use the vehicle under specific conditions with a particular end date that the car is to be returned. Franchising works in the same way. Franchising allows another investor or entrepreneur to purchase the rights to your company trade name and the use of your business processes or systems so that they can operate a similar business.

Franchising is regulated nationally by the Federal Trade Commission, and about half of the states in the USA have some additional compliance. You are required to have a Uniform Franchise Disclosure Document (UFDD) before selling a franchise. A lot goes into franchising a business. Our company offers a free consultation for anyone considering franchising their business.

### *The relationship*

The people involved in the franchise relationship include the franchisor and the franchisee. The franchisor is the person or company that owns the intellectual property, which consists of the brand name and systems. The franchisee is the person or company that purchases the rights to use the brand name and systems (think of it as a lease). Arguably the most critical word in this discussion is *relationship.*

When franchising your business, remember that this is *not* just business. This is a relationship between two people. The relationship needs to be more collaborative and structured as peers and not a parent-child relationship. If you are franchising your business expecting to be the ultimate authority and rule with an iron fist, you should reconsider franchising or change your mindset.

### *The Fees*

The franchisor generates its revenue in four primary areas: franchise fees, royalties, product sales, and other fees.

### *Franchise fee*

The franchise fee is the upfront fee a franchisee will pay you as the franchisor. Franchise fees typically range between $15,000 and $50,000. However, there is no requirement to fall within this range. Some franchisors charge nothing for a franchise fee, and other franchisors charge more than $1 million. There are many factors to consider when setting your franchise fee. Think of the franchise fee like operating cash flow for a new franchisor.

*Royalty*

The royalty fee is typically a weekly or monthly fee the franchisee will pay to the franchisor. It is generally a percentage of top-line revenue ranging from 1% up to 25% depending on the franchise system. The average royalty tends to be around 6% of gross sales.

The royalty is the real wealth builder for you as a franchisor and is often referred to as the get-rich-slow mechanism. A get-rich-quick mindset is wrong for running a franchise company, and if you plan to make a bunch of money in two or three years and move on, then franchising is probably not the right fit for you. If you have a long-term mindset and think about franchising as a long-term wealth-building vehicle, it can be personally, professionally, and financially rewarding.

*Product sales*

As a franchisor, you can sell to your franchisees various products needed to run and operate the business. If you decide to sell products, consider balancing profit for the franchisor and reducing costs for a franchisee. Many times franchisees join a system for bulk purchasing discounts. Consider how you intend to offer reduced prices to your franchisees. An ideal situation is that you are able to offer a noticeably below market rate for the product(s) and still have a profit margin. Remember that revenue from products or services sold to franchisees must be disclosed in the Uniform Franchise Disclosure Document.

*Other fees*

There is a myriad of other fees a franchisor might collect, including national marketing fees, technology fees, service fees, invoicing and collections fees, and many other services a franchisor might offer to a franchisee. The main takeaway is to be thoughtful and considerate when exploring which fees to charge and the price.

**Why Franchising Makes Sense**

Franchising your business makes sense because you can capitalize on three basics: 1. Money. 2. Management. 3. Multiply. Reviewing how one or all of these might impact your business will help determine if you want to consider franchising.

*Money*

The franchisee invests their money and financial resources to open up the franchise. This means they will be risking their financial assets, not you. Using other people's money to grow your business reduces your risk and allows you to have more locations/territories open.

*Management*

The constraints in the labor market seem always to be prevalent. Hiring and finding great employees is often the top challenge of running a business. By selling a franchise, you pass that burden to the franchisee to manage and operate their local franchise business.

### *Multiply*

Franchising takes you out of growth through an addition mindset and moves you into growth through a multiplication mindset. The shift is significant and allows you to grow faster in a much shorter period of time because each franchisee can be viewed as a micro investor to open and operate a franchise.

### The Triple Win Formula for Franchise Wealth Building

When you franchise your business, you are creating a residual revenue stream through a shared revenue model. When franchising is done well, it creates a win-win-win for the franchisee, the customer, and the franchisor. When this Triple Win Formula is applied, and all stakeholders receive their win, the whole franchise model becomes magical.

### *The franchisee win*

The franchisee wins when they have been trained on how to operate the business and successfully open. The franchisee also wins when the franchisor provides ongoing support to help the franchisees. The need for the franchisee changes over time as they mature as owners in the system. Ultimately, a profitable franchisee who is able to build the lifestyle they want through your franchise system should be a primary goal for franchisors.

## *The customer wins*

The customer wins in the franchise relationship when they are able to have a consistent experience at any franchise. The success for a customer is when they can expect to have the same quality service, quality product, or quality experience no matter which franchise location they visit. Whether it is a fixed location franchise or service based franchise.

## *The franchisor wins*

The franchisor wins when they receive their royalty payments and the franchise system grows in units and overall systemwide gross revenue. The franchisor also wins by making a positive impact in the lives of the franchisees, the customers of the brand, and the communities being served by the franchisees. The final outcome for the franchisor is the creation of a valuable asset to retain or sell.

## **Creating an Exit Strategy**

Franchising your business provides a pathway to create a sustainable long-term income stream as well as an exit strategy. Many clients I have worked with over the years are tired of working in their business but are not ready to give up the business they have built. This is where franchising can become an amazing solution. Franchising allows you to capitalize on your intellectual property and turn in to a franchise coach or a franchise trainer. You are also able to create an opportunity to sell your business for 6x, 8x, 12x eventually, or you might get lucky and sell for as high as 20x EBITDA (earnings before interest, taxes, depreciation and amortization).

## Become a Coach by Exiting Operations

Franchising your business will allow you to exit the daily operations of your business and focus on running your franchise enterprise. The franchisees will run their day-to-day operations, and you will provide support in the background to coach your franchisees. If you have thought about teaching, coaching, or consulting at some point, then franchising can provide you with a great opportunity to do that.

## Residual Income Stream

Some clients we work with are most interested in the long-term residual income stream franchising provides. These clients are interested in helping the franchisees succeed so that they can create much more predictable income to the business and themselves personally.

## Selling Your Business

When you franchise your business, the royalty revenue of the franchise company is viewed more like an annuity to potential investors and acquisition companies. The franchise agreement is typically a long-term contract that provides potential acquirers with confidence and security that they will see long-term dividends from the investment. In today's world, private equity investors purchase or invest in franchise systems with as few as 5 to 10 franchises. Private equity groups are running out of suitable franchisor investment options, so there is high demand and low supply right now.

**Conclusion**

Franchising your business and creating true wealth is feasible when executed well. Working with great consultants such as my company, Big Sky Franchise Team, great franchise lawyers, and other franchise professionals to support your growth will narrow your path to get there. Implementing the Triple Win Formula will provide you with the greatest chance to create wealth for your eventual exit out of the business as well as creating success and satisfaction for your franchisees and your franchisees' customers. Win-win thinking will go a long way in creating a sustainable and sellable enterprise to create the wealth and lifestyle you may seek through franchising.

# SCHUYLER "ROCKY" REIDEL

Managing Attorney, Reidel Law Firm
https://www.reidellawfirm.com/
Schuyler@reidellawfirm.com

832-510-3292

Schuyler Reidel is the founder and managing attorney for Reidel Law Firm. He started the firm in 2014 with a vision to provide valuable, cost-effective counsel to business owners in Texas. As the firm grew, he expanded the practice to bring his personable and accessible brand of counsel to include franchise law and international trade matters. While the firm is based in Galveston, Texas, where he grew up, he is often found traveling for business events and assisting clients around the world. If not in Texas, he is most likely to be found in Panama, United Arab Emirates, or Zambia.

Reidel has many friends, colleagues, and trusted resources. When he is not helping clients build successful businesses, he enjoys hiking, fishing, sailing, chess, and amateur fencing. He currently resides in Galveston, Texas, with his lovely wife after graduating from University of Arkansas-Little Rock's Bowen School of Law and Sam Houston State University with a public relations degree.

# Multi-Unit Franchise Ownership: The Key to Unlocking Generational Wealth

Multi-unit franchise ownership is one of the smartest and most secure ways to build wealth for yourself and your family. It's also a great way to ensure that your legacy lives on through future generations. Here's why multi-unit franchise ownership is so important, and how you can get started in this type of business today.

Multi-unit franchise ownership offers many benefits that individual franchise ownership does not. For one, it allows you to spread your risk across multiple locations and businesses. This diversification is crucial in today's ever-changing economy. By owning multiple franchises, you'll be able to weather any storm that comes your way.

Another benefit of multi-unit franchise ownership is that it gives you more buying power. When you own multiple franchises, you can negotiate better deals with suppliers and vendors. This can save you a lot of money in the long run, which can be reinvested back into your business.

Perhaps most importantly, the ownership of a multi-unit franchise, is a great way to ensure that your wealth is passed down to future generations. When you own multiple franchises, you can gift or sell franchises to your children or grandchildren. This is a fantastic way to help them get started in life and set them up for success. Naturally, if you have multiple units or concepts it can be easier for your children or heirs to make decisions on who should operate what. Some of your heirs may only want to be nominally involved while others want full operational control to build their own vision. Having multiple units can easily facilitate this with equitable division of your estate.

If you're interested in multi-unit franchise ownership, there are a few things you need to know. First, you'll need to find the right franchisor. Not all franchisors offer the same opportunities or support. Make sure you do your research and choose a franchisor that you can trust. Be sure to consult with franchise professionals like a franchise broker or consultant to guide you through the available opportunities and what would be the best fit for you. Additionally, you should sit down with a franchise attorney to fully understand the franchise agreement as a legal contract and your expectations and obligations.

Second, you'll need to have a solid business plan. This plan should include your financial goals, as well as a detailed marketing and operations strategy. Without a well-thought-out plan, it will be difficult to succeed in the competitive world of franchising. Many systems and nearly all banks will require a solid and well developed business plan before working with you. You will also need to find the right financing.

When you're ready to purchase multiple franchises, you'll need to have the capital to do so. There are a number of ways to finance your business, so be sure to explore all of your options.

Finally, you'll need to be prepared for the long-term. Multi-unit franchise ownership isn't a get-rich-quick scheme; it takes hard work and dedication to make it successful. Investing in your business today sets you up for success tomorrow, so don't be afraid to put in the extra effort. Consider the amount of work it will take to successfully operate a single unit of a franchise concept, now multiply it. Don't despair! Put in the hard work and develop a long lasting legacy for yourself and your family. Multi-unit franchise ownership is a great way to build wealth and ensure that your legacy lives on.

## What is multi-unit franchise ownership and why should you consider it for your business growth strategy?

Multi-unit franchise ownership is a business model where a single franchisee owns and operates two or more franchises of the same brand. Did you know: That most franchisees now are actually multi-unit operators, 54% of all franchisees, according to the International Franchise Association (IFA). There are several reasons why multi-unit ownership can be a winning solution for building wealth and passing wealth onto future generations. First, owning multiple units allows for economies of scale, which can lead to increased profitability. Additionally, by diversifying your portfolio across different brands, you reduce your risk if one business were to fail. Finally, as the owner of multiple units, you have the opportunity to create jobs and contribute to your local community. If you're thinking about becoming a franchisee, it's important to consider multi-unit ownership as part of your growth strategy.

Multi-unit franchise ownership does not have to be within the same system although generally it can be easier to open multiple units of the same concept. Some of the largest franchisees in the country are actually multi-unit franchisees of multiple brands. The largest of these are even publicly traded companies. For example, the Flynn Restaurant Group owns over 1,000 units in multiple brands such as Applebee's, Taco Bell, and Arby's and employ over 48,000 people in over 30 states. Another multi-unit titan is Sun Holdings, which started with a single Golden Corral location. They now operate over 1,000 units including Popeyes, Burger King, Arby's, and Papa John's.

When it comes to multi-unit franchise ownership, there are a few things to keep in mind. First, it's important to make sure that each unit is performing well. If one unit is struggling, it can have a negative impact on the entire business. You may end up in a situation where your successful units are subsidizing unsuccessful units which ultimately restricts your free cash flow and expansion capital. Additionally, multi-unit franchisees need to make sure that they have the necessary skills and resources for managing multiple businesses. You should be prepared to trust and delegate tasks and work to your team members so you can focus on the higher level management. You can't be in the back kitchen every day as a multi-unit franchisee. You must have a good management system in place so that you can effectively oversee all of your units.

This is also related to another important point that you need to have access to adequate capital to correctly staff and operate your units, even in the first few years. When you are a single unit franchisee it is much easier to bootstrap and step in when needed but this will not be possible with multiple units. It's important to plan ahead when opening additional units and consider the costs associated with expansion and operations across units. This may be challenging at first while your units build their cash flow but it is critically important to expanding sustainably.

**Keys to success when franchising multiple units**

1. Consult with experts at every stage of the process.
2. Make sure each unit is performing well.
3. Diversify your locations and brands in time.
4. Budget appropriately for multi-unit ownership.
5. Have a good management system in place. Delegate!

**How to get started in multi-unit franchise ownership.**

If you're looking to build your wealth and secure your financial future, multi-unit franchise ownership may be the answer. Not only does this type of ownership provide stability and a reliable income stream, but it can also be a valuable tool for passing on that wealth to future generations. Here are four steps to get started.

**Research:** Before taking the leap into multi-unit franchise ownership, explore all of your available options by researching different franchises and weighing their individual pros and cons. Consider both, franchisors' reputation and track record, as well as the potential cost to become a franchisee. It is also very important to consider the business potential and projections for a franchise unit in your market. Where in the past grossing $1 million would be a successful single unit franchise operations in many markets with a healthy profit margin, now with higher labor and cost of goods, margins are tighter than ever and you may need to be grossing $1.5 or even $2 million to be able to generate a healthy return and also fund future multi-unit expansion successfully.

**Financing:** Multi-unit franchise ownership isn't a quick process and requires significant start-up capital. It is important to plan ahead, keep your finances in order, and be sure to explore all financing options to make the most informed decision possible. One important thing to consider when financing a multi-unit franchise is the potential for economies of scale. When you own multiple units, you can spread your overhead costs (such as office space, marketing, and employee training) across all of your units, which can help to increase your profitability. Though economy of scale can be helpful in your expansion, keep in mind your capital costs will increase with each unit you develop. It will be imperative that you are well capitalized from the outset, do not try to bootstrap your multi-unit operations.

**Planning:** Once you have made the decision to expand into multi-unit ownership and have secured the necessary financing, it is important to create a detailed business plan that lays out your expansion strategy.

This plan should include information on each of your proposed units, such as projected sales and profits, as well as timelines for opening each unit. Will you develop within a single brand at first? Or will you explore single unit ownership in a handful of concepts at first. Will your unit placement be concentrated in a certain area or region? Most multi-unit franchisees do start within a single concept initially, either as a single unit or a multi-unit franchisee/developer. It is also important to have a solid management team in place who can oversee your expanding empire. You will be delegating most if not all day to day unit operations as a multi-unit franchisee.

**Location:** Choosing the right location for your multi-unit franchise units can have dramatic impacts on your success. Consider the local demographics and research what type of franchise would be the best fit for a particular area. Often with a multi-unit deal with a franchise system will be limited to a specific area or territory. It is imperative that this territory be adequate to fuel future growth while not cannibalizing your existing units. You should seek to negotiate and secure the right territory size for any franchise deal (multi-unit or not) you move forward with.

**Execution:** Finally, it's time to put your plan into action! Be sure to stay organized and keep track of all pertinent deadlines and milestones. As your business grows, it will be more important than ever to maintain high standards of quality and customer service across all of your units. With careful planning and execution, multi-unit franchise ownership can be a powerful tool for building wealth and passing it down to future generations.

**Legal Matters and Support:** As with any business, legal work is essential. A franchise attorney can provide critical guidance during the process to ensure you have a thorough understanding of the agreement and what it entails, from understanding your legal obligations to assisting with the various legal issues (leases, vendor contracts, employment matters, etc.) that come up in your business. Keep a franchise attorney close! Once you've become an official multi-unit franchise owner, don't forget that franchisors offer ongoing support. This may vary from system to system but you should take advantage of the insight and direction the franchisor offers.

Multi-unit franchise ownership is a great way to start building long-term wealth and financial security. With research, planning, financing, the right support, you can turn your dreams of business success into reality. Start your journey and become the multi-unit franchise owner you've always wanted to be!

**Things to keep in mind when expanding your business through multi-unit franchise ownership.**

In order to expand your business through multi-unit franchise ownership, keep the following in mind:

1. Make sure you have a solid business model that can be replicated in multiple locations.
2. Choose a strong franchise system with a good track record of success.
3. Do your due diligence and research the potential market for your business before investing.
4. Plan ahead and allocate the necessary resources upfront in order to be successful.
5. Have a financial plan in place that takes into account future growth potential.

6. Understand the legal requirements for multi-unit franchise ownership.
7. Hire experienced professionals to help oversee the operations of your businesses.

Multi-unit franchise ownership can be a great way to build wealth and pass it on to future generations. It is important to take the necessary steps in order to properly plan and execute this type of business expansion. By paying attention to these key considerations, you will set yourself up for success as a multi-unit franchise owner.

**The key to unlocking generational wealth.**

Multi-unit franchise ownership is the key to unlocking generational wealth. By owning multiple units of a franchise, you can build up your income and assets over time, eventually handing down that wealth to future generations. This is an important strategy for those looking to achieve financial stability and security in the franchising industry. It is not only a great opportunity for franchisees to increase their wealth, but it can also be beneficial for those hoping to become franchisees in the future. With the right knowledge and resources, multi-unit franchise ownership can provide a strong foundation for building and passing along lasting financial success.

**Case studies of multi-unit franchise owners who have achieved great success.**

Multi-unit franchise ownership can be a successful way to build wealth and pass it down to future generations.

The key is finding the right franchise system with a proven track record of success. Here are two case studies of multi-unit franchise owners who have achieved success in multi-unit franchise ownership (names identifying information changed for privacy):

### Case Study 1: John and Sue Sampson

John and Sue Sampson are a husband and wife team who own three Subway franchises in their hometown. They started out with one location in 2016, and expanded to two locations in 2019. Their third location opened in 2021. The Sampsons have been able to grow their business by leveraging their combined skills and strengths. John is responsible for the day-to-day operations, while Sue handles the marketing and financial planning.

The Sampsons are a great example of how multi-unit ownership can be a winning solution for building wealth and passing it down to future generations. By owning three Subway franchises, they have been able to create a stable income stream that will provide for their family for many years to come. What's more, they have been able to do all this while maintaining a high level of control over their business.

Eventually, their plan will be to either pass on the business to their two children or to sell the business and retire on the proceeds.

### Case Study 2: Bill and Karen Brees

Bill and Karen Brees are the owners of six McDonald's franchises in upstate New York. They started out with one location in 1993, and expanded to six locations over the next 20 years. The Brees have been able to grow their business by focusing on quality customer service and by keeping their costs low.

Like the Sampsons, the Brees are a great example of how multi-unit ownership can be a winning solution for building wealth and passing it down to future generations. With six McDonald's franchises to their name, the family has been able establish themselves as successful business owners with the freedom that brings. In addition, they have achieved this while maintaining control over operations and making sure that everything is going well internally at all times!

**FAQs about multi-unit franchise ownership**

1. **What is multi-unit franchise ownership?**
   Multi-unit franchise ownership refers to the ownership of multiple franchises within the same franchise system.
2. **Why is multi-unit franchise ownership a good idea?**
   Multi-unit ownership can be a great way to build wealth and pass it down to future generations. By owning multiple franchises, you can create a stable income stream that will provide for your family for many years to come. It becomes easier to leverage your investment and assets for continued growth with each franchise unit.

3. **What are the benefits of multi-unit ownership?**
   The benefits of multi-unit ownership include:
   — Increased income potential
   — More control over your business
   — Higher quality standards
   — Greater stability and security

4. **How do I get started in multi-unit ownership?**
   The best way to get started in multi-unit ownership is to find a successful franchise system with a proven track record of success. Talk to other owners in the system and get their advice on what has worked for them. Consult with franchise consultants, brokers, and a franchise attorney as well.

5. **What are the risks of multi-unit ownership?**
   The risks of multi-unit ownership include:
   — Increased risk if one or more of the franchises fails, especially if you have not adequately hedged your risk with diverse systems and locations
   — More time and effort required to manage multiple locations
   — Increased financial commitment

6. **What are the costs associated with multi-unit ownership?**
   The costs associated with multi-unit ownership vary depending on the franchise system you choose. However, you can expect to pay a higher initial fee and more initial capital costs than you would for a single franchise.

7. **How can I make sure my multi-unit ownership venture is successful?** To make sure your multi-unit venture is successful, you need to focus on quality customer service and keep your costs low. You should also be prepared to devote more time and effort to managing your multiple locations.
8. **Can I own multiple franchises in different markets?** Yes, you can own multiple franchises in different markets as long as you have negotiated that right in your franchise agreement and the markets are available in the franchise system. You should take steps to secure the right territory in any franchise you consider joining.
9. **What happens if one of my franchises fails?** If one of your franchises fails, you will be responsible for the financial losses incurred by that franchise. This may include any loans, vendor contracts, liquidated damages, or personal guarantees that you have been contractually obligated for. However, you will still have the other franchises to fall back on.
10. **How much time and effort do I need to devote to managing my multi-unit franchise venture?** It depends on the franchise system in particular but you will need to devote a significant amount of time and effort to managing your multiple locations. In addition, you will need to be prepared to make a significant financial commitment to your venture.

11. **What is the best way to find a good franchise system for multi-unit ownership?** The best way to find a good franchise system for multi-unit ownership is to talk to other owners in the system and get their advice on what has worked for them. You should also look for a franchise system with a proven track record of success. A great way to get help with this is utilizing a franchise broker or consultant in your search.

12. **How much money do I need to start a multi-unit ownership venture?** The amount of money you need to start a multi-unit ownership venture varies depending on the franchise system you choose. Be sure to review Item 7 of the Franchise Disclosure Document. However, you can expect to pay a higher initial fee and a higher royalty rate than you would for a single franchise.

13. **Can I own multiple franchises in different industries?**
Typically, yes you can only multiple franchises in the same industry but they should not be competitors. For example you should not expect to be a Papa John's franchisee and a Domino's franchisee, but owning both a Papa John's and a Subway will usually be permitted.

## GREG AGUIRRE

https://capitalrivers.com
greg@capitalrivers.com
info@capitalrivers.com

**O**: 916-514-5225
**M**: 916-804-8046

Greg Aguirre is the CEO of Capital Rivers Commercial (www.capitalrivers.com) and is a senior level commercial real estate expert in acquisitions, leasing, contract negotiations, entitlements, portfolio management, and ground up development. Prior to founding Capital Rivers Commercial in 2015, Aguirre spent over 15 years on the corporate real estate side of the industry working directly for companies including CVS/pharmacy, J.P. Morgan Chase, and the Sleep Train group of companies. Capital Rivers Commercial is a full service commercial real estate firm specializing in site selection, tenant representation, real estate development, and asset management.

At Capital Rivers Commercial we help franchisees maximize their investment by including real estate as part of their strategy. We love discussing commercial real estate, especially when it comes to franchisees and franchisors.

# Maximizing Wealth: The Synergy of Franchise Ownership and Commercial Real Estate Investment

Building wealth through franchise ownership and commercial real estate can be achieved by leveraging the strengths of both investments; however, it requires a combination of strategic planning, smart investments, and disciplined execution.

### Pros and Cons of Buying vs. Leasing Space as a Franchise Operator

Buying vs. leasing space as a franchise operator is a complex decision that requires careful consideration of multiple factors. Both options have their advantages and disadvantages, and the best choice depends on the specific needs and circumstances of the franchisee. Here are some of the pros and cons of each option:

**Pros of Buying:**

1. Control: This is probably the No. 1 benefit of owning the real estate where the business operates. Commercial real estate ownership provides the franchise owner with complete control over how the property is used, managed, and maintained.

2. Appreciation: Commercial real estate has the potential to appreciate over time, providing owners with long-term capital appreciation. This can lead to significant financial gains, especially if the property is well-located and well-maintained.
3. Income Generation: Commercial real estate can provide a steady stream of revenue through rental income. If the franchisee is operating in a portion of the property and can collect rent from other tenants this could help provide additional revenue and financial stability.
4. Equity: The franchise operator can build equity over time through the repayment of the mortgage vs. simply paying rent to a landlord. If the franchise owner sells the business in the future, they can hold onto the real estate and lease the space to the future franchise owner while continuing to build equity.
5. Tax Benefits: Commercial real estate ownership provides several tax benefits, including deductions for mortgage interest, depreciation, and property taxes. These deductions can significantly reduce your tax liability, freeing up more capital for reinvestment in the business.
6. Real Estate Finance: The ability to utilize real estate and business finance strategies, such as borrowing against the equity in your real estate portfolio, to fund expansion and new investment opportunities. As an owner-user you may also have access to more favorable financing options

such as the Small Business Administration (SBA) 504 loan.

The SBA 504 loan program is a loan program offered by the Small Business Administration (SBA) to provide small businesses with long-term, fixed-rate financing for the purchase or development of commercial real estate. The SBA 504 program is designed to help small businesses grow and create jobs by providing them with access to low-cost financing for real estate projects. The SBA 504 loan program is structured as a partnership between the SBA, a private lender, and the borrower. The SBA provides a portion of the financing, typically 40%, while the private lender provides 50% and the borrower provides the remaining 10%. The private lender also serves as the primary lender and is responsible for underwriting the loan and servicing the debt.

Benefits of the SBA 504 loan program include:

1. **Low Down Payment:** The SBA 504 loan program allows small businesses to purchase or develop commercial real estate with a low down payment, typically 10%.
2. **Long-Term Fixed Rates:** The SBA 504 loan program provides long-term, fixed-rate financing, which helps small businesses budget for future expenses and reduces the risk of interest rate fluctuations.

3. **Lower Cost:** The SBA 504 loan program provides low-cost financing compared to traditional commercial real estate loans. To be eligible for an SBA 504 loan, a small business must meet the SBAs size standards, be a for-profit business, and typically have a tangible net worth of less than $15 million and an average net income after taxes for the two full fiscal years prior to the application of less than $5 million. Additionally, the business must occupy at least 51% of the commercial real estate property. If you're interested in obtaining an SBA 504 loan, it's important to work with a lender that specializes in SBA loans and has experience in the 504-loan program. They can help you navigate the application process and provide guidance on the best loan structure for your specific needs. Visit www.sba.gov to learn more.
**TIP:** When considering an SBA 504 loan make sure to research a good Certified Development Company (CDC) to help you navigate the process. 504 loans are available through Certified Development Companies (CDCs), SBAs community-based partners who regulate nonprofits and promote economic development within their communities. CDCs are certified and regulated by the SBA. Small business applicants work directly with a participating SBA lender and not with SBA.

7. **Legacy Building:** Commercial real estate ownership can provide owners with the opportunity to build a legacy that can be passed down to future generations even if the future generation isn't interested in continuing to run the franchise business. This can provide owners with a sense of pride and fulfillment, as they contribute to their family's financial security and prosperity.

**Cons of Buying:**

1. **Initial Cost:** The upfront cost of buying the property can be substantial and may require a significant investment of capital. This could impact the amount of capital the franchisee could utilize to grow the business.
2. **Maintenance Costs:** As the owner of the property, the franchise operator will now be responsible for all maintenance and repair costs, which can be expensive. Typically, the tenant is paying a lot of these expenses as additional rent in the form of Common Area Maintenance (CAM) reimbursements including taxes and insurance all of which are considered the triple net expenses (NNN). The difference is that as the owner you will be responsible for managing all of it in addition to necessary capital improvements such as roof replacement, parking lot replacement, etc.
3. **Lack of flexibility:** Once the franchise operator purchases the property, they are essentially

committed to it, and if their business needs change it can be challenging to sell the property and find a new location. It's important to consider the uniqueness of the business and long-term viability of the location. For example, a fast-food restaurant that as a prototype design and that requires a drive-thru will likely not need to relocate in the near-future and the real estate will likely maintain its future value provided the quality of the real estate and market are solid.

**Pros of Leasing Space:**

1. **Lower Upfront Costs:** Leasing a space requires a much lower upfront investment than buying, making it a more accessible option for many franchise operators.
2. **Reduced Responsibility:** When leasing a space, the franchise operator is typically not responsible for the maintenance and repair obligations outside of their physical space.
3. **Flexibility:** Leasing a space provides the franchise operator with greater flexibility, as they can choose to renew their lease or move to a new location if the business needs change.

**Cons of Leasing Space:**

1. **Lack of ownership:** Leasing a space does not provide the franchise operator with the benefits of

ownership so they don't have the opportunity to build equity over time. The payments go towards rental payments, not ownership of the property.
2. **Limited control:** As a tenant, the franchise operator has limited control over the property, and they must typically seek permission from the landlord to make any changes or improvements. There can also often be restrictions within the lease, including but not limited to, inability to sell certain products, limitations on type and/or style of signage, restrictive operating covenants. i.e.: limitations on parking, operating hours, etc.
3. **Limited tax benefits:** Tax benefits associated with owning commercial property, such as deductions for mortgage interest, are not available when leasing.
4. **Uncertainty:** When the lease term expires the landlord could re-negotiate the lease terms, including increasing the rent or terminating the lease if they have a better tenant.

On a larger scale, think back to what McDonald's founder Ray Kroc said in 1974: "I'm not in the hamburger business, my business is real estate." He believed that the key to success in the fast-food industry was to have the right location. This meant the property needed to be highly visible, easily accessible, and on high traffic arterials so it was convenient to customers. This also typically is the criteria for a lot of other retailers and or what makes for a valuable real estate site.

In summary, Ray Kroc's philosophy on real estate was that the right location was the most important factor in success of a business, and that owning property was essential in order to maximize the value of that location. On a smaller scale, an independent fast-food franchisee looking to secure the real estate as part of their expansion plans can leverage the brand name and strength of the franchise concept to secure the real estate through the following strategies:

1. Development through ground-up construction.
2. Acquisition and retrofit of an existing building.
3. Lease the real estate and secure an option to acquire the real estate at an agreed upon date (Purchase Option) or secure a Right of First Refusal (ROFR) to purchase the property before it is sold to a third party.

The franchisee would then build the business and increase the EBITDA, sell the business at a multiple, and retain the real estate.

- Sell the business at a multiple
- Retain the real estate
- Lease the real estate back to whoever it is that purchased the business. This will provide a lump-sum cash from the sale, which can be used to invest in additional real estate properties or other investments.

- Secure new financing, if appropriate based on the current lending environment, and cash-out on the increased equity resulting from the new long-term lease.
- Collect rent from the tenant (new business owner).

**Tip:** When negotiating the new lease with the prospective new business owner (Buyer) it is important to consult with an experienced commercial broker and attorney to maximize the value of the asset. For example, you should look at the length of the lease term, frequency of rent increases, who is responsible for what operating costs Triple Net Expenses (NNN's), in addition to other lease provisions.

EBITDA stands for Earnings Before Interest, Taxes, Depreciation, and Amortization. It is a financial metric used to measure a company's operating performance and is calculated as revenue minus expenses, excluding interest, taxes, depreciation, and amortization.

This business owner could now potentially make more money on the real estate side over time than they would from the initial sale of the business. But remember: the primary focus starting off in franchise investments should be building a successful sustainable business.

There are a few questions an investor (the franchisee) should ask themselves before signing a lease or buying commercial real estate:

- Is the investment financially sound? I.e., is enough revenue generated to have a positive cash flow, a

healthy balance sheet, and the ability to generate sufficient income to support its operations and long-term goals.
- What is best for the long-term success of the franchisee business and the brand?
- Is this the best location to be successful in the short and long-term?
- What is my anticipated after-tax cash flow?
- What is an appropriate Occupancy Cost to sales ratio for the business?

Occupancy Cost refers to the total cost of occupying a commercial property, including rent, property taxes, insurance, maintenance, and any other expenses related to the property. It is a key factor to consider when evaluating the financial viability of a commercial real estate investment or leasing a property for business purposes.

Occupancy cost can have a significant impact on a business' bottom line, so it is important to consider all costs associated with a property before making a decision. A property with a lower occupancy cost can provide cost savings and allow a business to allocate more resources to other areas, while a property with a high occupancy cost can put a strain on a business' finances.

To determine the occupancy cost of a property, you should consider factors such as the size of the property, its location, the length of the lease, and the terms of the lease agreement. You should also factor in potential expenses such as property taxes, insurance, and maintenance costs. It is important to review the lease agreement carefully and understand all the costs involved before making a decision. In summary, occupancy cost is a crucial factor to consider when evaluating commercial real estate investments or leasing a property for business purposes, as it can have a significant impact on a business' finances.

**Teamwork:** When you consider buying or leasing a a commercial property, it's critical for you to build a team of professionals to help make informed decisions. At a minimum, the following individuals should be a part of that team:

1. an experienced real estate broker with strong relationships
2. a tax advisor
3. an accountant
4. a capital market advisor

Working with franchisees and franchisors is a big part of what we do at Capital Rivers Commercial. As a commercial real estate firm, we work collaboratively with the franchisors and franchisees to help them find the real estate that best fits their own unique business model. Every business is different and because of this, we strive to understand the inner workings of each business.

This type of attention to detail allows us to give our clients the competitive advantage in an ever-changing commercial real estate marketplace. We are able to create a purposeful expansion strategy and customized site criteria created by using existing customer data as well as other technology tools such as artificial intelligence tools (a.i.). In addition, we negotiate specific lease structures and/or purchase agreements that support our clients' unique business goals to ensure long-term success. Capital Rivers Commercial frequently acts to bridge the gap between the franchisors and franchisees with clear communication and a detailed and defined strategy. The franchisor wins when the franchisee is successful, which includes paying royalties and representing the brand appropriately. Success is achieved by both parties when it is truly a team effort.

The following are important points for Capital Rivers Commercial to consider when working with a franchisor or franchisee.

- Detailed understanding of the "brand" including its origin, purpose, and culture.
- Detailed understanding of the financial operation of the business.
- Detailed growth development "Roll-Out Plan" for the current year and subsequent years.
- Detailed analysis of critical real estate criteria specific to the brand, including demographic analysis, traffic study, co-tenancy study, traffic generators, etc.

Greg Aguirre, CEO of Capital Rivers Commercial, started his career in commercial real estate after graduating from Sacramento State's College of Business Administration/Real Estate and Land Use Affairs Program. In his first 10 years after graduation, he worked in corporate real estate for companies like Armstrong Development, J.P. Morgan Chase & Co., and Sleep Train.

Later on, he founded Capital Rivers Commercial, a commercial real estate brokerage, development, and property management firm that has quickly become an industry leader by combining technology with traditional work values. While in college, Aguirre was determined to break into the industry, so he completed multiple internships, including ones at Centex Homes and Grubb & Ellis, and took the necessary classes to earn his real estate license. To support himself financially, he researched property ownership, visited the planning department and local title companies, attended meetings, knocked on doors, sent letters, and did everything else he could to sell in-fill development property to a local home builder.

Currently, Aguirre is a senior-level commercial real estate expert in acquisitions, leasing, contract negotiations, entitlements, portfolio management, and ground-up development. Capital Rivers Commercial, which he founded in 2015, is a full-service commercial real estate firm that specializes in site selection, tenant representation, real estate development, and asset management. The company is committed to providing the highest level of service and using innovative techniques to meet clients' needs.

Join us as we dive deeper into building wealth through franchise ownership and commercial real estate. Connect with us at www.capitalrivers.com to participate in meaningful conversations, exchange valuable insights, share contacts, and provide answers to your questions as we work together to pave the way for success in the world of commercial real estate and franchise ownership.

# TONI HARRIS TAYLOR

DrasticResults.com
NIAGlobalPartners.com
Toni@NetworkinAction.com

713-387-9273

Toni Harris Taylor is the award-winning franchise owner of Network in Action Global Partners. NIA Global Partners is an international community of business owners who come together to mastermind and grow their business, bring each other warm referrals and a supportive community for one another. Toni lives by the mantra of being DRASTIC! In her business, Drastic Results Marketing and Sales Coaching, she helps her clients learn the strategies to get known, get connected and get paid to make six figures and beyond. Toni is an 8x author and most recently her collaboration project, Viral Networking for Drastic Results™ achieved Amazon International Bestselling status in Sales and Marketing categories. Toni is a Videocast show host, a philanthropist, and has won several awards for her work including, NIA's first Rookie of the Year (2019), Brand Ambassador (2021), and the 2022 Power Networker of the Year from Dr. George C. Fraser, proving Toni knows networking!

# From Quitting to Legacy

Have you ever been at a crossroads where you didn't know which way to go? Seriously, like one of those decisions that if you make a choice it could change the trajectory of your life in a positive way or put you in the place of misery. Either choice is scary and can change your life drastically. Speaking of drastic, my coaching business, Drastic Results Marketing and Sales Coaching, is all about helping entrepreneurs to get out of their comfort zone and helping entrepreneurs stay in business through networking and building key relationships. My slogan is "Get known, get connected, and get paid." I have a passion for helping entrepreneurs to be drastic, getting out of their comfort zone and being who they need to be so they can have what they want to have.

In 2019, I was standing at that crossroad and faced with a monumental decision that could make or break my future. I was close to leaving my coaching business. It wasn't because I wasn't making money. I was a six-figure business coach, coaching my clients who were having drastic success. But I couldn't see how to scale and grow my business so that it would be saleable in the future. I thought I needed to quit my business to get a job. Now let's be clear, I did not want a job, but that's all I could envision to create a retirement plan. I spoke to Carol, a networking friend who's a money mindset coach. After explaining my predicament, she asked me, "Toni, what's your why?" I told her my why at that time and she said, "You've already accomplished that. Perhaps you need a new why. One that will inspire you to want to stay in business." She said, "I want you to pretend you don't have a business and create a new why, then come back and tell me what it is." A few weeks later, I had my new "why," my purpose.

I told her, "My why is to touch, move and inspire my clients to take drastic steps to be better than they were before they met me. I'm a resource, I'm a connector. I want to help people build deeper relationships that are beneficial to their life and business."

She said, "That's perfect for you." What would you need to do to get paid to connect people?"

I said, "I would need to start my own networking group."

"Why don't you?" she asked.

I chuckled and said, "Absolutely not! There is no way. I've seen too many people run networking groups and not make any money. I don't know what to charge. I don't have technology. I don't know how to run a meeting. No thank you."

She said "Toni, if that truly is your why, don't worry about how the solution will show up."

A week later, Helen, from Network in Action followed up with me. I had met Helen at a women's retreat three months prior while I was contemplating getting a job. Helen said, "Toni, do you remember me? I haven't forgotten about you. I still think you should be a Network in Action franchisee." I thought to myself, *I forgot about you. Just last week I said no way to starting a networking group.* I went straight to the money.

"How much is that franchise again?" I asked.

She told me and I responded, "I don't have that kind of money."

She encouraged me, "Just meet the franchisor."

I pushed back and emphasized, "Helen, I really don't have that kind of money. I don't want to waste his time. Besides, I'm waiting for two job offers."

She insisted, "Just meet him."

I agreed to meet Scott Talley, the Network in Action founder and visionary. Our connection was instant. He even had a payment plan for the franchise fee. I asked him if the franchise was saleable (my number one concern with my coaching business) and he said yes.

After much contemplation and discussion, I took the drastic step and signed on the dotted line. It was a D-R-A-S-T-I-C step, and I was petrified! However, I was more petrified to take a job. Sometimes you must be more afraid of what happens if you don't take the risk.

I realize that most people are safe and comfortable where they are, but nobody gets to their next level staying inside their comfort zone. Taking that first drastic step, getting out of their comfort zone so you can see what's on the other side. We must let go of what's safe and there's a lot of fear in that. We know fear is false evidence appearing real, but most things that people fear never, ever, come true. Now, follow me. I go from interviewing for jobs, about to quit my business, to signing for a franchise? Scared to death was an understatement for what I was embarking on. In my self-talk, I said, "What the heck are you doing? What if it doesn't work?"

Six months, after purchasing the franchise, the COVID-19 pandemic hits. Now our in-person networking must go online. Fortunately, I was already an online networker, so it was easy for me to lead my members into the virtual networking space. In hindsight, COVID-19 was one of the best things that happened to my franchise. It gave me the opportunity to expand our network from beyond the borders of Northeast Houston to go global. In October 2021, our franchisor added virtual groups to our business model and the world became our territory.

**Drastic Results + NIA = A Perfect Combination**

When NIA came into my life, I knew it was the right fit because it complimented exactly what I was already teaching my coaching clients. I teach my clients marketing and sales strategies. The number one strategy I teach is networking the *right way*. In Drastic Results, I teach people how to network with NIA, and I give them a place to network. In 2021, I decided to create The Viral Networking Conference, where I emphasized the power of networking and suddenly it all fit together like pieces of a puzzle. Imagine having all these pieces and watching them come together. The picture became so much clearer of what I'm meant to do, who I'm meant to serve, how I'm meant to serve them.

**Scaling Up**

After being a franchise owner for two years, I felt like my franchise still wasn't scaled. I am determined to have a business that can run without me. I started looking at the model and thinking, "What if I could do this by bringing in other people to start groups around the world?" I see a lot of people volunteering to be the president of BNI or someone else's association as volunteer chapter presidents. I asked myself, *What if I paid people to build these groups around the world? Then I would have a real true scaled and saleable business model.* I knew that to have a business that runs without me, duplication would be the key.

As I write about it, I marvel at how God put all these things in place when I couldn't see what was ahead of me. NIA strengthened my coaching business 10 times. If you are a business coach, NIA is a perfect companion to what you are already doing. It is my goal to reach more business coaches with this method and help them to see how being an NIA leader or franchisee can help them grow their coaching business. I really want to help them to see that. It goes hand in hand with what we do.

Even though I have a great plan for duplication, it hasn't come without challenges. In January 2022, I brought on six leaders. Six leaders went through training, and two of them disappeared. They didn't even communicate with me. So that left four. Of the four, two of them have had difficulty bringing on new members. One of them got cancer. I added a couple more leaders, and one month later, one of those new leader's daughter was killed in a car accident. Life has got in the way of my plan every time I bring on new leaders.

The other big challenge is finding people who are as passionate as I am about networking and connecting people. I know what networking can do for people's lives, but not everybody is convinced. I put people through the process, and it's been a little bit challenging to find the right fit. Here's what I know. I'm improving as a leader to ask the right questions, find the right people, and to coach them through their life challenges. I know for sure at the end of the day my goals will be met, and the leader's goals will be met if I stay focused on helping them to reach their goals.

What did Zig Ziglar say? "You can have everything in life you want if you help enough people get what they want." That's what I'm focused on. Even though there have been challenges, it's going to be just fine and it's coming together. What I love about what I'm building is I'm not alone and we are doing it together. The leader who lost her daughter, said most of her support has come from the NIA family and she had only been a part of NIA for just a few months. The franchisor flew to Baltimore and visited her during this time.

One of the best stories come from two of my members, one from Houston and the other from Virginia who both didn't understand the power of networking but joined NIA anyway. When my leader's daughter died, the Houston member happened to be traveling to Virginia to visit family. The second member, in Virginia, got together and drove an hour and a half to sit with my leader in Baltimore, to love on her. That made me proud. I know I'm on the right path when I know our community is there to support people in their darkest hours. I often say that people join for business, and they become family. The lady from Houston was not going to renew her Network in

Action membership after her first year. I convinced her to stay and focus on building relationships. She said "Toni, I don't need friends, I need to write business."

I told her "When you make friends, you will write more business." From that point, her business changed drastically and now, two years later, she is traveling to another city to comfort somebody she met three weeks prior, and she was happy to do it out of love.

Another success story is of a partnership that came out of Network in Action. My virtual group is the Network in Action National Networkers. Two of the members, one a branding expert and the other a content writer, grew their relationship to form a partnership. One evening about nine o'clock at night, the content writer texted me and said, "Hey, if you've got a minute, I want to share some exciting news." She called me and I could hear the excitement in her voice, She said, "Oh my gosh, I just closed my first five figure content deal."

I said, "Really? Tell me more."

She said, "Yeah, it was through the branding expert in our NIA group. We partnered together on her client and the deal was done!" The slogan for NIA is "Building Relationships that Last a Lifetime," and no matter what happens to me in the future, my members will be friends forever. That is the legacy that I'm leaving.

### Leaving a Legacy

When I started my coaching business, I knew I wanted to leave a legacy of drastic steppers who get out of their comfort zones and learn how to network and teach their kids how to network so that their kids don't have to struggle with submitting resumes that go into a black hole. If their kids want to have a business, they can teach their kids how to network because they learned from me how to network the right way. I discovered that I could use my franchise to leave a legacy when I started bringing leaders onto the team. My goal is to have more than 20 leaders that have 24 members which extends the family globally.

There are two additional ways that Network in Action is helping me establish a legacy. The first way is through community service. I never knew how giving back is good for business. I have the privilege of gifting a nonprofit membership in each group. I've seen how the nonprofits have been able to flourish as a result. One of my nonprofit members, who was new to Houston, joined NIA in November 2021. He had a gala in April 2022 with over 200 people. Most of them were NIA members.

We have another nonprofit member called the Prison Entrepreneurship Program. Our members are privileged to volunteer inside the prison and coach them on strategies for their business plan competition. One gentleman, who was released from prison with a message he wants to get out to the world, is now an NIA member and coaching client. I will help him launch his speaking business. Community service is a huge advantage of becoming an NIA franchisee that I didn't see coming. If I can teach my leaders to bring on a nonprofit, and get involved, that's going to extend their business tremendously.

Community service was not a natural thing for me, I will give the franchise credit for introducing me to the power of community service and bringing that nugget into my life. NIA helped me to see how doing good for others is truly good for business. A second way I'm building legacy is purchasing the appropriate life insurance for my family since NIA has helped me more than double my income. I will leave a financial legacy for my family tax-free. I would like to offer my D.R.A.S.T.I.C. steps to using franchising to build a legacy.

1. **D**etermine your goals. I knew I wanted a scalable, saleable business for the future. I went into the NIA franchise with those goals in mind and the NIA business model allows for the ability to reach those goals.
2. **R**isk is important to reward. To create a legacy, you must take the risk. Buying one unit is not likely to create a legacy but creates more of a job for you. The real way to build a legacy is to take the risk and duplicate with buying more than one unit.
3. **A**ction to move forward. When NIA came into my life, I had to take action to purchase the franchise. Then I had to go to work to build the franchise. When COVID-19 hit, I had to take drastic action to keep my members engaged.
4. **S**ervice. I've learned that having a community service and give back strategy helps businesses to grow. Implementing a community service plan will help you to build a legacy because you are touching people beyond your franchise.
5. **T**ake your time but don't delay. I keep reminding myself that Rome wasn't built in a day. I thought it

would only take me one year to have 20 leaders. I didn't realize the challenges that would come along the way. I've decided to slow down and be more selective about the leaders that I bring on, but I'm not stopping and I'm even more determined to make it happen no matter what!

6. Invest in yourself and your business. Continue to keep learning. Invest in networking so that you can meet people who know people, places, and things that you don't. Study your craft. Invest in your people to help them to grow too. Don't look at the expansion of your franchise as an expense but understand that it is an investment in your future legacy.

7. Commitment. Stay committed to the process. I've had challenges expanding my franchise and bringing on leaders, but I'm committed to making it happen. My commitment is bigger than just me. It is also a commitment to the leaders and their future members that we haven't met yet. With my plan to expand, it will touch so many entrepreneurs and help them to grow their businesses globally.

I never saw myself owning a franchise. I did not see it coming and wouldn't trade it for anything. Now I own eleven units! Franchising has changed my life. I'm an advocate for franchising, especially for minorities and women. The more people I can encourage to get into franchising, and enter with legacy building on their mind, buying multiple units, doing the right thing with the money, giving back, then everybody wins.

# DAVID & LAURA GREENWOOD

www.owlbetherefranchise.com

Laura.Greenwood@owlbethere.com
David.Greenwood@owlbethere.com

1-218-OWL-CARE (1-218-695-2273)

David and Laura Greenwood began Owl Be There in the Washington, D.C. market in 2013. They had a passion to provide "wise guidance" to seniors and their families - and a combined thirty-five years of business experience. It wasn't long before David needed to add more senior advisory experts to his team to handle the growing client base.

With the confidence that Owl Be There's values and processes could be replicated in other markets, the Greenwoods launched their franchise system in 2020. The business is flourishing, and they look forward to welcoming many more dedicated, caring franchise owners to the Owl Be There family in the coming years.

"We are 'all in' on training and coaching and are dedicated to making owners profitable and confident. They train right alongside our amazing executive senior advisory team and participate in the process in real time—even before opening their local business."
—**Laura Greenwood**

This husband-and-wife team draws on their broad business backgrounds to make Owl Be There a well-rounded organization. David has an MBA from Georgetown University and worked for a decade in financial services guiding families in wealth management and long-term care planning. He went on to become Salesman of the Year at a national healthcare company in 2012 and has trained dozens of top performing salespeople across the country. He loves coaching and advising– particularly in the senior space where he found his calling. David also enjoys playing the piano and singing the national anthem at sporting events and minor league baseball games.

Laura received her MBA from The College of William & Mary and is a Certified Franchise Executive. Her background includes product management, consumer advertising, corporate strategy and financial planning and analysis at a $2 billion organization. She is passionate about marketing, operations and franchise growth strategy. Laura also loves cooking, gardening, volunteering at her sons' schools and golfing.

The Greenwoods live in Northern Virginia with their two sons and one very spoiled cat.

# Make a Great Living While Making a Difference

Not long ago, while working at a large internationally recognized nonprofit organization, I had a conversation with one of my employees about mission. It was his first full time job and, like many college graduates new to the world of employment, he was curious about how soon he could expect to be promoted.

While this question was not unusual or unexpected, the turn of the conversation revealed a cultural shift that many nonprofits struggle with today.

Traditionally, nonprofits attract employees and volunteers who are driven by the power of "The Mission," with financial gain or professional advancement taking somewhat of a back seat.

In fact, many nonprofit organizations rely on this altruism for survival; it's incredibly difficult for some nonprofits to compete with the higher salaries and attractive bonuses that for-profit companies can offer. So, his response to my next tried-and-true talking point ("You get to support an amazing mission!") stopped me short:

"That's true. But I can do charity work in my spare time."

Honest. Blunt. Pragmatic.

A few months later, though he sincerely believed in the organization's mission, he left for a large salary bump at a for-profit company nearby. In fact, several employees left for more lucrative opportunities at for-profits in the months that followed.

Supporting a noble mission was admirable, but ultimately wasn't paying the bills. And maybe he was right: A win for "The Mission" shouldn't come at the expense of those fulfilling it day in and day out. This is why David and I are so proud to offer a franchise opportunity that combines an extraordinary mission with business scalability and the opportunity to grow personal—even generational-wealth.

It's true, you really can make a great living while making a tangible, compassionate difference in the lives of senior adults. Allow us to introduce you to Owl Be There.

## WHAT IS OWL BE THERE?

Owl Be There provides senior living referral and advisory services to seniors who need home care, assisted living or memory/dementia care. We come alongside seniors and their families with the goal of lowering their stress by educating and advising them on the many available options.

We help them through the process of finding viable solutions that meet their price range, level of care need, and other requirements. There is never a charge to seniors or their families for working with Owl Be There.

We are compensated by our network of communities when a senior chooses one and moves in.

And every time that happens…

- a senior receives safety and care
- a referral partner's client receives concierge-level service
- a senior living community receives an ideal resident
- a franchise owner is well compensated and appreciated and
- Owl Be There's mission to improve lives is fulfilled once again.

Can you name another career or franchise opportunity that provides a "win-win-win-win-win" for all stakeholders?

## JUST CALL AND "OWL BE THERE." WILL YOU?

The senior population is growing in the U.S. That's no secret. Here are a couple of U.S. census statistics to add some color and context to that fact.

- Ten thousand people in the United States turn 65 every day; By 2030 – practically right around the corner – that will mean one in five people will be over age 65.
- Forty million "baby boomers" will join the senior ranks by 2030, swelling the total U.S. senior population to over 75,000,000.

This "silver tsunami" is a huge and growing market segment, and it is projected to continue growing for the next one to two decades. In terms of senior living and care, the senior population boom is driving a couple things.

First, it is responsible for the recent flurry of senior and assisted living facilities being built up around the country. I would be willing to bet you've seen some of these huge building projects in your own neighborhood or city. After all, the U.S. assisted living facility market size was valued at $91.8 Billion in 2022 and is projected to grow 5.5% year over year through the next decade.

Second, it has driven a proliferation of options and more specialization in senior living and care options than ever before; Alzheimer's, Parkinson's, and Lewy body dementia care to name a few. The result is better, more personalized, condition-specific care solutions.

But having more options also presents a bigger challenge for families. Which communities and services are appropriate for my senior loved one? Is there a room available? How much will it cost? What medical requirements and logistical hoops must we navigate before mom or dad can move in? How do we even begin to figure this all out?

**Enter Owl Be There!**

All of that growth, unfilled capacity and choice translates to immense opportunity for what Owl Be There has to offer – both for seniors needing care and for aspiring business owners who are ready to take charge of their careers. Franchisees are perfectly positioned to forge relationships in their own communities, make a real difference in peoples' lives, grow their business, and build their personal wealth in the process.

And I haven't even mentioned the freedom of being your own boss and setting your own schedule. Or the low investment and expense profile of a home-based business.

Which begs the question, how do you know a superior franchise opportunity when you see one?

## HOW TO IDENTIFY A GREAT BUSINESS OPPORTUNITY

Since you are reading about franchise opportunities to build personal wealth you are already on the right track. And since you've made it this far into our chapter, I am going to assume you are a mission-driven leader with a heart for helping seniors and a desire to set your own priorities, schedule and wealth goals.

You may have heard the old adage that franchising means you are in business for yourself... and not by yourself. It's actually true.

When you invest in a franchise opportunity, your risk is greatly reduced. Robust support systems and resources are available to you. The painful (and often painfully expensive) trial and error stage is foregone; All of the 'newbie' mistakes have been made by the franchise founders and recorded as cautionary tales in the Best Practices manual for your edification. The kinks have been worked out; secrets to success have been discovered, developed and documented; and systems have been put in place to help increase productivity and keep the whole thing organized and on track. Finally, the business model is proven, successful and profitable.

Those attributes and benefits should be a given for any great business opportunity, and they are at Owl Be There. Our team has decades of senior industry experience and a love for coaching, training and celebrating franchisee successes. We have a deep passion for equipping, training and mentoring entrepreneurs in the senior advisory space.

But beyond what's been put in place by the franchisor, if you wanted to dive into a new career that will provide success and build security and wealth for you and your loved ones, you would look for an opportunity with the following key attributes:

**First, look for a business in a market segment that is growing (or booming!)**

The unprecedented growth of the U.S. senior population is driving massive expansion in the senior housing and care space. Assisted living and senior care services aren't new or trendy, and they aren't going to be outmoded or commoditized. People continue to age and need personalized care.

Medical science continues to advance and develop treatments and therapies that extend and improve lives. Adult children continue to move away from home, establish dual-career families, and generally create "overscheduled" lives–which limits their ability to take in and care for senior family members. Given all of these trends, the need for knowledgeable advisors to help families understand senior housing and care options will continue to grow as well. Demand is on your side!

**Next, look for a business that provides something truly needed or essential.**

Non-essential businesses perform well in non-pandemic and economically secure times, but services that are in demand regardless of external forces will experience less volatility and revenue risk. Owl Be There provides essential guidance to a growing segment of seniors and their loved ones. There is no high-quality substitute for the empathy, kindness and advice our franchisees give to seniors who desperately need a solution in short order.

**It is also a good idea to find a business that requires a low initial investment and low ongoing expenses.**

This allows you to become profitable more quickly and stay profitable as you invest in and grow your business. A home-based business that requires no buildout, rent, equipment or inventory – like an Owl Be There franchise – is a low-cost opportunity that sets owners up for early financial success.

Since the recent pandemic, business owners and employees alike have discovered a new appreciation and expectation for a more flexible work-life balance. If you've left a stressful 9-to-5 office existence with a grueling commute, there's no reason to land in a similar situation you'll regret. Being your own boss, setting your own schedule and appointments, giving yourself the freedom to…brace yourself… run errands, volunteer at your child's school or grab some "me" time to keep your balance and rejuvenate—that is the stuff of home-based, owner-operator dreams. It's also how Owl Be There owners live life every day!

**Finally, and this one is absolutely essential, find a business that satisfies your personal sense of mission.**

If you have a heart for making a difference in people's lives, and that's what you do all day every day, you'll be motivated and inspired, and ultimately very successful in your career; You will make a great living while making a difference. You will receive amazing feedback from your clients, including notes and emails filled with gratifying statements like "I don't know what we would have done without your help. Thank you so much!"

What if you could get all of these things wrapped up in a single opportunity: a growth market, rising demand for your essential service, low cost to drive early profitability, leadership control and a flexible work-life balance, and a mission that inspires you to get up in the morning and give it your all? And what if you could access world-class training, operational and CRM platforms, innovative marketing programs, and ongoing support to get you up and running in weeks—instead of years? We would love to show you how.

## FRANCHISE THROUGH THE FEAR

I know what some of you are thinking. *All that sounds great, but I've never run a business before. I'm not sure this is a risk I'm willing to take.* I get it. I really do. Let me share a little more of our Owl Be There story with you.

David and I are similar in many ways…and in other ways complete opposites. Between the two of us, he is the visionary. David is the one willing to try things and take risks, and he believes most things will work out if you just give it your all, despite any roadblocks and limitations you encounter along the way.

Me, on the other hand… I'm "Ms. No." I am risk-averse and an analyst by nature. When I hear a plan, I am the one who tries to poke holes in it to make sure it is feasible (or discover that it's not).

I don't always have the big idea – but I love to figure out how to make the big ideas work. All I ever wanted was to work for an organization where I could do something interesting or worthwhile, and where I could rely on a 9-to-5 schedule, a steady paycheck, health insurance and, ideally, some level of 401(k) matching. No ups and downs or uncertainty. That was the life for me.

For decades, David had wanted to be in the world of franchising, but the right timing and opportunity never seemed to come along. It took a few years for me to warm to the idea of him owning and operating a franchise. His path had taken him through financial services, then sales for a national healthcare company, where he became Salesman of the Year.

To me that sounded like job security. To David that sounded like it was time to move on. And move on he did. Right into building his own business from scratch: "feet on the street," forging relationships and helping seniors find assisted living options that were right for them.

It took some time (I still refer to that time as "the nail-biter years"), but it wasn't long before he was making a name for himself in the Washington, D.C. metropolitan area. Then he hired another senior living advisor to help handle the volume. And then he started trying to convince me this was a model we could franchise to not only help more seniors across the country, but to train and guide owner-operators to great success as well.

Of course, I said… "no." Too big. Too scary. Too expensive. Too much risk. What if it didn't work?

But David is persistent, and it helped that the business was growing by leaps and bounds. He finally talked me into taking some franchising courses at Georgetown University to get my feet wet and understand the potential of a solid franchise model.

I went on to become a Certified Franchise Executive and. Over the next couple of years, began using my spare time to help David set the groundwork for building a franchise system. We launched Owl Be There Franchising in 2020–and by mid-2022 there was more work than I could handle on nights and weekends.

It was time for me to make the (big, scary, risky) jump. I left behind a six-figure management position at a billion-dollar organization, a great team of colleagues, and all that perceived job security. And I haven't had time to look back or miss it – much to my surprise! Why am I telling you all of this? Merely to demonstrate that David and I understand the hesitation one might feel when thinking about leaving what is safe and familiar to build something new. It takes courage. But by investing in both yourself and a proven franchise model, it may also be an opportunity to take your career to a fresh new level. You won't miss the old one. You'll be too busy doing something you love and making a huge difference—every day—in the lives of seniors in your community. You'll build, grow and scale. You'll set your own schedule and have time to run errands, volunteer, and work from pretty much anywhere.

The reason Owl Be There is so focused on mentoring and individualized training is because we know, personally, the challenge of "changing the channel" in the middle of your career program. Every franchisee has a different path and a unique set of valuable experiences they will leverage to grow their new business. Our design is for franchise owners to get all the training they need for a fast start, and then receive further support and mentoring to refine, problem solve and fill experience gaps as they grow and thrive. Franchise owner success is our success. It's as simple as that.

## LOOKING FOR LEADERS WITH A HEART FOR SENIORS

I've never met anyone who was looking forward to leaving their home and entering an assisted living community. Not one person. Many senior adults today still think of assisted living as "the home," or "the nursing home"–the one place you don't want to end up. Of course, today's assisted living and memory care communities are not the facilities of yesteryear. Some of them can best be described as "a cruise ship on land" with a wide variety of meal choices, resident activities and services, and even regular excursions and outings to local events.

Nevertheless, everyone wishes to stay in their family home as long as they can. Many families whose elder members need support start out with in-home caregivers. But they soon realize that home care can, in a very short period of time, become terribly expensive. Often, this course of care services is not sustainable, and the family is once again in need of a workable care solution.

That is why it is so important to us to find franchisees with a heart and desire to help vulnerable seniors find the care they need, within their budget, and in an environment where they can find comfort and society. The franchise owner comes alongside the distressed family with empathy, patience and confidence that they can help. Their advice is welcomed and appreciated.

The first question we always get is "Do you have to have a senior care background to become an Owl Be There franchisee?"

The short answer is "no." While some franchisees come to us from the senior care industry– or from experience like hospice care or senior facility management–it is not a requirement.

What's more important is that you want to help, and you have a strong desire to improve the lives of seniors. The details around how to do that can be learned.

That said, skills like people management, leadership, sales, or previous business ownership can be very helpful in this role. As the fundamental focus is on quality guidance, someone who likes to lead, educate or coach others will likely be a great fit.

## OPPORTUNITY AND GROWTH

Choosing a care solution for mom or dad is, in many ways, a very emotional decision for families. The Owl Be There senior advisor's role is to educate the family on all the good choices that are available in the local marketplace, not pressure them to go in a certain direction. That's one unique thing about a service like Owl Be There: we advise on all care options.

For example, you may have a senior who needs care and has the resources to engage in-home care services instead of going to assisted living. The home care option is a revenue stream for the franchisee just as much as any other care solution.

Home care, assisted living, memory care, a temporary respite stay–even independent senior living–all are viable revenue stream opportunities that the franchise owner can access just by helping families go in whichever direction they feel is best for them.

Another way Owl Be There bolsters a franchise owner's opportunity is through robust territories. When we find someone who discovers that owning an Owl Be There franchise is the right move for them, we build a robust territory around their home location and personal and professional network.

We start with a minimum population of 400,000. Then we assess the number of large and small assisted living communities, hospitals, rehabilitation facilities, and other senior referral sources in the territory. This helps us to identify the potential for the business to flourish, scale, and grow for years to come.

The future franchisee can also request that specific locations or zip codes be included in the territory design, and Owl Be There often is able to accommodate those preferences. It's much more of a flexible collaboration than a "territory in a box." Owl Be There also has relationships with national and regional senior living companies that franchisees may have access to in their own territory, giving them a head start on options for placing seniors on day one!

While we expect owners to be engaged full time running their business, they may also discover the need to add one or more staff members as their business scales up after the first year or so. The option of investing in additional territories is also available. At Owl Be There we are flexible in working with our franchise family's aspirations and goals.

But mostly, we are excited for the opportunity to train, equip and empower new business owners to make a huge difference in people's lives—including their own! When you are inspired and invigorated by the work you do and the positive impact you have on others, your "work" becomes a big part of your life's "balance." So, whether your ideal opportunity is with Owl Be There or another franchise that aligns with your personal mission and growth goals, we suggest you dive in and thrive!

# LINDA BALLESTEROS

Linda@MpowerFranchiseConsulting.com
www.mpowerfranchiseconsulting.com
https://www.linkedin.com/in/lindaballesteros/

832-640-4922

Linda Ballesteros, (pronounced By-yes-TED-os) is a certified franchise consultant who helps aspiring entrepreneurs find the best franchise opportunities for their goals and budget. Whether you are looking for a low-cost, home-based, or high-growth franchise, Linda can guide you through the process of finding, evaluating, and securing the right one for you. Linda is passionate about franchising and loves to share her knowledge and expertise with others. She is also a professional life coach, goal setting coach, mindfullness coach, law of attraction coach and a career coach.

Linda is a speaker, an international best selling author and the host of All Things Franchising Radio Show.

If you are ready to take the next step in your career and become your own boss, contact Linda today and let her help you find the opportunity that will help you build full spectrum wealth!

# Seeking Full Spectrum Wealth

Definition of wealth –

A great quantity of money, valuable possessions, property, or other riches.

All things that have a monetary or exchange value.

Knowing the definition of wealth is meaningless unless you know YOUR definition of wealth.

Money is one form of wealth, however, how valuable is it without your health or family and friends to enjoy it with? It is wonderful to have the finances, family/friends and good health but full spectrum wealth would also include the time freedom to go to the gym, take a vacation with the family or to attend your child's little league games.

Let's start with identifying the four spectrums of life:

1. Health
2. Relationships
3. Time
4. Financial

Without balance in all four quadrants, reaching your goals will be a struggle and you most likely will feel less than fulfilled at the end of the day.

**WHY HEALTH IS YOUR GREATEST WEALTH**

A Roman poet said "The greatest wealth is health." So, this isn't a new concept.

Recognizing the direct link between health and wealth should be a part of your plan in seeking full spectrum wealth. We tend to take our good health for granted until we come face to face with a situation that brings our attention back to the basics of living a healthy lifestyle.

Here are a few tips you can easily incorporate into your life:

**Water**
Drink enough water to maintain the body's fluid balance, which helps transport nutrients in the body, regulate body temperature, and digest food.

**Exercise**
Regular exercising burns calories and helps you manage your weight. Exercise prevents coronary heart disease, stroke, diabetes, obesity, and high blood pressure.

**Think positively**
Positive thinking turns all problems into opportunities; it can improve the immune system functions and decrease blood pressure. People who have positive thoughts make better decisions and have more confidence in themselves.

*Without our health ... we are nothing.*

We strive for personal success often at the expense of our health. For some, the value of their health is only recognized once it is at jeopardy.

Making other things a priority over health and taking our bodies for granted impacts our ability to create wealth.

Taking good care of your health could be challenging but it is an important component to full spectrum wealth.

## RICH RELATIONSHIPS

One of the pillars of true wealth is the way you relate to people. Not only with your family, but also with your community, your friends and colleagues/employees.

You will never feel truly wealthy if you don't have loving people around you. My definition of a rich relationship is one where both people feel valued and respected. They listen, support, challenge and disagree with each other however they still do great work together.

People who have healthy relationships are more likely to feel happier and satisfied with their lives.

**Kushal's Story…**

Kushal was a successful Wall Street analyst who had just entered the doors of the second twin tower on 9/11 when it got hit. As he describes in his best-selling book, *On a Wing and a Prayer*, his brush with death was a wakeup call. Having a career where he mainly focused on financial wealth acquisition before 9/11, he began to question his life's purpose.

This new perspective completely changed his relationship with his employees. In the past, his leadership style had been primarily transactional. After 9/11, he started seeing his employees as individuals, each with their own unique set of strengths and needs. He began to lead with compassion, kindness, and authenticity instead of only focusing on efficiency and how each employee impacted the "bottom line." This change allowed him to feel more present and whole as a person than ever before. Kushal eventually left his corporate career to start his own business venture which skyrocketed.

He became a serial entrepreneur with multiple successful endeavors and sold his first venture for $15 million. His latest venture is a successful pro-social enterprise that donates 25% of its profits to childhood education in India.

Whether you are a business owner or have a corporate position, you are building relationships so make each and everyone special.

## CREATING TIME WEALTH

Have you ever heard the phrase…"Money rich and time poor?"

This describes people who have relatively little leisure time despite having a high disposable income.

Many people accept time poverty as part of the corporate job. Some have tried to solve the problem through a variety of flexible working arrangements especially since COVID, however their time still belongs to their employer.

What I have noticed is that since the pandemic, more people experienced less stress and more happiness by stepping off of the corporate rat race.

What is the price of working 70 hours a week to support a lifestyle you can't participate in.

### Bill's Story

Bill came out of a successful 25 year career in corporate America. He had made the sacrifices and put in the work necessary to achieve the title of VP of Sales that hung on the door to his office. Along with the title was the unspoken obligation to work late nights and weekends. Whether those hours were spent working on the next big deal, the department's success or mentoring a junior team member, his chair at the family dinner was empty.

Make your time memorable by making it meaningful. Be intentional when creating your calendar activities. Put personal and family events a priority by placing them on your calendar.

Time poverty does not have to be the default setting. More time freedom allows space for the creative mind and solutions/ideas flow easier.

Embracing a time freedom abundant mindset inspires us providing us with a reason to jump out of bed each morning. Don't postpone the things that light you up and make life meaningful.

### WANT FINANCIAL WEALTH?

Unfortunately, only a fraction of the people who aspire to be wealthy will actually be successful. There are many paths to building wealth, from starting your own business to investing in the stock market, but no matter which path you choose, there are some specific financial fundamentals you'll need to master before you can take the next step.

## Wealth is a Mindset

> "I am a rich man. And rich men don't do that."
> —**Robert Kiyosaki**

Like many now-wealthy individuals, Robert Kiyosaki from the *Rich Dad Poor Dad* books once found himself completely broke. In addition, one of his failed businesses had left him over $1 million dollars in debt.

He knew he could throw up his hands and give up on ever building wealth again. But he didn't.

"I am a rich man — and rich men don't do that!"

Despite the big "$0" in his bank account, his mindset of wealth remained stronger than ever. He has since amassed hundreds of millions of dollars through his "Rich Dad Poor Dad" curriculum.

**Building massive wealth rarely happens unless you have a firm belief that you can do it.**

Building massive wealth starts with your mindset and a focus on full spectrum wealth. If you believe you can get rich, you're far more likely to succeed than someone who doesn't really believe it.

### Don't listen to the majority

That's because the majority of people aren't wealthy. Most people are broke, in debt, have poor financial behaviors and overall unhealthy habits. Most people overspend, don't save, don't invest, don't develop their financial intelligence and live unbalanced lives.

Think of the most common financial advice you've probably heard over the years. It probably includes recommendations like:

Save your money
Get a good job with a good paycheck
Diversify your portfolio
Be frugal
Don't take big financial risks
Your home is your biggest asset
Pay off your credit card every month

But according to the world's most influential financial books, this advice is usually *bogus*. One of the most common characteristics of massively wealth individuals is that they typically go *against the tide* of mainstream financial behavior.

**Make your money work for you**

Most people trade time for money. They don't know how to make their time and money work for them.

Every dollar is like a little seed that can grow and sprout more dollars. This is the essence of having "money work for you." Every dollar not "planted" was a waste of a seed that might eventually blossom into a massive money tree. You need to plant your dollars.

**Mary's Story...**

Mary had worked in a corporate position for 20+ years always getting praise for her dedication plus getting raises and bonuses along the way. One day she walked into her boss's office to announce that she was leaving. She had no response when he started questioning where she was going and what her plans were. All she knew is that there had to be a better way.

Striking out on her own, she discovered talents, skills and interested in areas that made her very marketable. This translated into building a business where she earned more than what her corporate position could have ever delivered. Her newfound excitement and confidence created a wealth mindset which was reflected in her bank account.

Don't follow traditional advice…it's usually not helpful. This is why the clients I work with are drawn to franchise and business opportunities that give them the freedom to own their own business by following a proven program. There are some risks with any new business however working with a company that is by your side, will set you up to be successful.

The secret is to finding the concept that will cash in on your talents and encourage you to never stop investing in yourself. Following these fundamentals won't guarantee wealth, however it will open the door for new possibilities.

## FULL SPECTRUM WEALTH OPTIONS

You may evaluate your current situation and determine that with a few "tweaks" you can begin living a wealthy life.

Others may need to implement a few major changes however are able to see the possibility of living a full spectrum life. Then there are those who just don't know where to begin.

As a franchise consultant, I find great joy in helping clients in each of these categories to truly experience wealth in all areas of their lives.

Discovery is the first step to opening the door to what can be by exploring your options.

> "The biggest adventure you can take
> is to live the life of your dreams."
> **—Michael Jordan**

Made in the USA
Middletown, DE
27 August 2023